INTRODUCTION TO

Keats

By the same author

THE USE OF IMAGINATION
Educational Thought and the Literary Mind

A HUMAN IDIOM
Literature and Humanity

COLERIDGE
The Work and the Relevance

A MANIFOLD VOICE
Studies in Commonwealth Literature

V. S. NAIPAUL

COMMONWEALTH LITERATURE

READINGS IN COMMONWEALTH LITERATURE (editor)

D. J. ENRIGHT
Poet of Humanism

PATRICK WHITE: VOSS

PATRICK WHITE'S FICTION

F. R. LEAVIS

INTRODUCTION TO

Keats

WILLIAM WALSH
Professor of Commonwealth Literature
and Douglas Grant Fellow
in the University of Leeds

METHUEN
LONDON AND NEW YORK

First published in 1981 by
Methuen & Co. Ltd
11 New Fetter Lane, London EC4P 4EE

Published in the USA by
Methuen & Co.
in association with Methuen, Inc.
733 Third Avenue, New York, NY 10017

Typeset by Scarborough Typesetting Services
Printed in the United States of America

British Library Cataloguing in Publication Data

Walsh, William, *b.1916*
Introduction to Keats.
1. Keats, John – Criticism and interpretation
I. Title
821′.7 PR4837 80-41754

ISBN 0-416-30490-7
ISBN 0-416-30500-8 (University paperbacks)

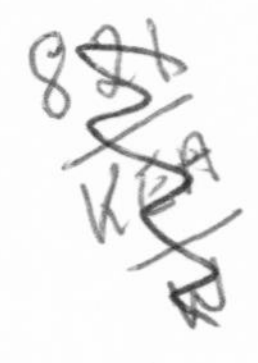

For my wife
Toosey May Watson Walsh

Contents

Foreword

Anyone who writes on Keats must be aware of the immense debt he owes to those who have written before him. I am deeply beholden first, to those who established Keats's text and made it available, and in particular to H. W. Garrod, Miriam Allott, Jack Stillinger and John Barnard; and secondly, to Keats's biographers, and especially to Robert Gittings and W. J. Bate. I am also profoundly conscious of an obligation to the devoted and imaginative scholarship of the editors of Keats's letters, Maurice Buxton Forman and Hyder Edward Rollins. The critics from whom I profited are named in the text. I am grateful to Chatto & Windus for allowing me to draw on my essay on Keats in *The Use of Imagination* (1959).

1
The opening sensibility

This book is meant for students – actual students, that is, in colleges and universities – and potential students, any general readers who see themselves in this modest role. What follows derives directly from my idea of what would be useful to such readers, given the aim of introducing them to the poetry of Keats. Such an approach implies certain assumptions about the proportion of biographical information to critical judgement, about the level of analytical sophistication to be aimed at, and about the best development and arrangement of the topics. I hope to have got this balance about right. My aim is to illuminate the poems, and indirectly the man, and more obliquely the period. This seems to me the best order of understanding and, indeed, one in my experience preferred by students.

Just as a literature is more than an array of individual works, composing an order expressing and helping to form a common mind, imagination, and sensibility, so the works of a great poet are more than a collection of single and separate pieces. They are bound together by their sources, their direction, their continuity and their purposes. Really to have grasped the significance of, and truly to have profited from the richness of the poet's experience, the student has to achieve that degree of insight which enables him, in a purely educative experience, to sense and respond to the organic unity of an *œuvre*. Getting a view of 'the figure in the carpet' is not done by attention to any general and abstract discourse, whether of a critical or philosophical or biographical kind, but by means of many immediate experiences of the concrete. I work, therefore, consistently from those immediate expressions of Keats's personal and artistic experiences, his letters and his poems, and hope thereby to apprehend myself, and make available to others, the clue to the allegory of Keats's life. He himself said, 'A man's life of any worth is a continual allegory – and very few eyes can see the

Mystery of his life – a life like the scriptures, figurative – which such people can no more make out than they can the Hebrew Bible. Lord Byron cuts a figure – but he is not figurative – Shakespeare led a life of Allegory; his works are the comments on it –.' Certain of Keats's poems, 'La Belle Dame sans Merci', 'The Eve of St Agnes', the 'Ode on a Grecian Urn', 'To Autumn', have been the initiating and moving first experiences of the poetic and literary life of so many. Such experiences are marked by intensity and concentration and it is in moments like these when emotion is powerful and distinct that taste is formed:

> preferences then grown conscious, judgments then put into words, will reverberate through calmer hours; they will constitute prejudices, habits of apperception, secret standards for all other beauties. A period of life in which such intuitions have been frequent may amass tastes and ideals sufficient for the rest of our days. . . . Half our standards come from our first masters, and the other half from our first loves.[1]

On these experiences – and they may be few – when they are crucial and alive, hang all our systematic opinions, and the enduring value of the latter depends on the degree in which they keep the former present and active. Keats's genius entitles him to be among the category of our first masters; his marvellously attractive and sympathetic character to belong to those in the second category. My purpose, then, is to analyse, justify and confirm these experiences in the learner's mind – when they have taken place; and when they haven't, to provoke and encourage them.

Introduction to Keats, it is hardly necessary to point out, is by no means a biography or even a biographical sketch. I have used the lightest of biographical scaffolding to support my account, a structure composed by the three volumes of poetry published in his life-time, together with the letters which discover the leading themes of his personal and artistic experiences. This simple arrangement is sufficient, I believe, to make chronological sense of Keats's development while saving the learner from being stupefied by an aggregation of merely biographical facts. For information about Keats's life I rely first on Keats's letters and then on the labours of others. I want to consider Keats's writings as comments on his life, that astonishing passage from cockney to classic. An essential clue to the understanding of his poetic life, to the interpretation of the 'allegory', is, it seems to me, an educational one, since Keats's career is the most brilliant example in literature of the education of a sensibility. Sensibility, an important if cloudy word, was not much used, the *Oxford English Dictionary* points out, until the middle of the eighteenth century. Addison had used it to imply quickness and acuteness of apprehension or feeling, and with Warton and Sterne it carries the sense of a capacity for refined emotion and delicacy of taste. In the nineteenth century it was used in a psychological sense to mean sensation or perception, or the readiness of an organ to respond to stimuli; or again in a philosophic sense, to indicate feeling as distinguished from cognition and will. I want to use it in a way which draws on each of these sources, and which has best been explained by Rémy de Gourmont: 'Par sensibilité j'entends, ici comme partout, le pouvoir général de sentir tel qu'il est inégalement développé en chaque être humain. La sensibilité comprend la raison elle-même, qui n'est que de la sensibilité cristallisée.' It is the maturing of such complex power that I have in mind when I speak of the education of sensibility – what Keats himself described as the effort 'to refine one's sensual vision into a sort of North Star'.

This is the formative and organizing intention of a study which is emphatically literary-critical in means and emphasis. I want to develop it in a setting which attempts to make clear the tone of Keats's society as well as the main events of his life; at the same time I shall endeavour to indicate and illustrate the shape and lineaments of Keats's character. Keats, who was in a formal sense the least well educated of the great Romantic poets, was an extraordinary and original genius, and by no means a simple follower of the earlier Romantics. It was he, for example, who inaugurated that literary movement, completed only in the time of Eliot, which finally 'dislodged' Milton as a principal creative influence on poetry in favour of Shakespeare. He was a man of unusual and peculiarly appealing character: exquisite aesthete and a lover of boxing; the son of a livery stable keeper, trained as a medical student and a qualified doctor from one of the best medical centres of the time, whose inner life was one of profound spirituality and imaginative vitality. He was gored by reviewers, whom he treated for the most part with mature disdain. He had a strong gift for intimate friendship with members of his own sex, and he had a sensuous and passionate nature of an orthodox heterosexual kind. He was at least once treated for gonorrhea with the then fashionable drug, mercury. His love for his brothers and sister, George, Tom and Fanny, was deep and self-sacrificing. A pugnacious bantam in boyhood, he was physically robust before he got the disease that killed him. He nursed his dying brother Tom devotedly. We can't say that he caught tuberculosis during this time – it was a year later that he had his first attack of blood-spitting – but the family predisposition to tuberculosis would not have been weakened by long hours of harassed attendance on the patient, and it was certainly then that he began to develop a chronic sore throat. His love affair with Fanny Brawne, whom he was never able to marry, was one of the most intense and tragic in literary history. He was not only a star-crossed and consumptive lover, who died in his twenty-sixth year of the tuberculosis that killed his mother and brother, but a potent creative genius of the first order. I should add that Keats is one of those very great men on whom there can be no final word said but towards whom every generation and every reader should attempt to define his relations anew.

John Keats lived for less than twenty-six years. He was born at the Swan and Hoop livery stables between Finsbury Place and London Wall on 31 October 1795 and he died in Rome in the Piazza di Spagna on 23 February 1821. That meagre stretch of life witnessed the unfolding of one of the most remarkable and attractive geniuses in English literature. It also took in one of the most fascinating periods of English history. There is a sense in which all those from Chaucer to Pope belonged to the same universe of thought, one informed by similar assumptions about God, order, and significance. Keats belongs to the period, the Regency, which finally sealed off that great span of history. After the Regency, we live in another world, a world of the individual consciousness and of fluid and uncertain categories of value, the world we ourselves substantially inhabit. The Regency saw the beginnings of urban and industrial society, and an agricultural system beginning to be penetrated by macadam roads and later by railways, altering irreversibly in favour of an industrial and factory economy. The country began to have a strongly commercial tone and bias. Britain was cut off from practical connection with Europe by the Napoleonic wars, but as we see in the case of Bentham and Coleridge, this did not mean the total disruption of intellectual influence: German idealism and French pragmatism strongly influenced the thought of these seminal minds of the period. It was certainly a period of creative energy in the arts, particularly in those of painting and literature, though less so perhaps in architecture, where the figures are of lesser significance: Nash, Soane, Wilkins, Smirke and Wyatt. But few periods can summon such a list of names in the other two arts: Jane Austen, Wordsworth, Coleridge, Bentham, Hazlitt, Constable and Turner, and to these we have to add the name of Keats.

The period was not only notable for its glittering collection of individual talents, but for the way in which the force of eighteenth-century value and style was being irresistibly sapped by the contrary forces of Evangelicalism and Utilitarianism. The Regency was as much a watershed of cultural history as the seventeenth century. It had a politically stable context. Lord Liverpool's administration though dull was strong and efficient.[2] Based on this sure ground the period itself gave off a sense of bubbling, even brutal vitality, such as we see even in the ordinary social life of Keats's lower-middle-class society. There are some remarks by Q. D. Leavis about the pre-Victorian England in which Dickens was reared which are peculiarly appropriate to the period of Keats's own upbringing:

> Dickens's was a pre-Victorian England of course, with the uninhibited licence of the Regency lower-middle-class. . . . Practical jokes of the most unrefined kind and even savagery, histrionics and travesty for fun, hoaxes or 'flams', uninhibited punning and broad jests, excessive tippling, as well as a now unknown degree of sentimental susceptibility, were characteristic of the age Dickens was formed in.[3]

Only the force of the beavering Bentham could finally tame it, and prepare the way for the more blanched gentility of the Victorian era. It was a time of immense wealth and economic strength and appalling injustice and misery for the poor. It is true that the state of the working class was probably less grim than it was to become in a fully industrialized Victorian Britain, and that its misery was being to some degree ameliorated by the innumerable self-help clubs and societies; by the beginnings of primary education under Bell and Lancaster, the Anglican version of which Coleridge, in one of his more idiotically sectarian moods, called 'an especial gift of Providence to the human race . . . this incomparable machine . . . this vast moral steam engine'; and by radical politics, whether of the more robustly working-class or the more gentle patrician sort. Probably no one then writing protested with more passion and point at the wretchedness of the poor than Coleridge,

Keats's great predecessor. Coleridge had as little respect as anyone for the 'Negative Pull down and Clear-away Principle'. But he detested the idolatry which acted as though 'by some pre-established harmony, some new refinement of predestination, a boorly soul was born a Boor – and that all calm and lofty souls entered into the foetuses of future Serene Highnesses'.[4] Coleridge raged against a country where healthy workers were called 'the labouring poor' or where people waxed complacent about the 'numerous soup-establishments', or where pieces of beef were hung up to attract the half-famished mechanic to the services; 'Fools! To commit robbery and get hung when they might fight for their king and country – yea, and have sixpence a day into the bargain', or where children from six to sixteen years stood for thirteen to fifteen hours in a heated and polluted atmosphere in the cotton factories. Those who expected such things, said Coleridge, must believe that 'all the opinions, concerning the laws of animal life, which have been hitherto received by mankind as undoubted truths, must be false: or else there is a continued interference of a miraculous power suspending and counter-acting those laws, in mark of God's especial favour towards the Cotton Factories.'[5]

Keats was as appalled by social misery as Coleridge, but his own politics were vaguer and less firmly organized than Coleridge's. They are more private and belong to the category of decent sentiment rather than party feeling. He was mildly sceptical, republican, leftish. Naturally he was against vulgar superstitition (as an early feeble poem shows) and political oppression (more consciously so when he was under the influence of Leigh Hunt); he was horrified by the savage poverty and the human degradation he saw among the Scottish and Irish peasants; he was against lords (particularly, indeed, six-foot lords, as his comment contrasting his treatment by the public with Byron's makes clear: 'You see what it is to be under 6 foot and not a Lord?'). But he was not a leveller or a philosophical radical. He was neither a foaming enthusiast nor one who saw the future as something to be determined by Benthamite statistics. As a poet he was too possessed by the tragic view of man; as a man his life was riven with too many tragedies.

Keats, of course, was not a member of the labouring poor, but of the modest middle class. I suppose in such a rigidly structured age he would have been thought of as belonging to the lower range of the middle class. The snobbish and bitchy *Blackwood's Edinburgh Magazine* picture of the starved and uneducated apothecary – the wavering apprentice anxious to quit the gallipots – had no relation either to his background or to his circumstances. He was the eldest of five children, of whom four survived. His father first worked in the livery business for John Jennings who had built it up, and then married the daughter of the family and himself became the manager. He was killed on 16 April 1804 in a fall from a horse. His mother, in circumstances of considerable ambiguity, married William Rawlings only two months after his father's death. (According to Keats's grouchy and irritable guardian-to-be, Abbey, Keats's father was drunk when he died and she was no better than she should be.) This enigmatic remarriage, which turned out to be a failure, had a profound effect on the life the family led. They had gone to live with their grandparents on their father's death and they were now really wholly in the charge of their grandmother, Alice Jennings, who was not only a grandmother but a sturdy, prudent, North Country grannie, who made over capital of some £8000 to be held in trust for the children. When the grandfather died the family moved to Edmonton. When, six years after her remarriage, Keats's mother, about whom he was to preserve an almost unbroken and surely significant silence, herself died of tuberculosis, it was a shattering experience for the boy who had nursed her with passionate devotion when he was on holiday from school. If Keats reported in himself in later life 'a horrid Morbidity of Temperament',[6] his beginnings would certainly justify it. 'I have never known any unalloy'd Happiness for many days together; the death or sickness of some one has always spoilt my hours.'[7] If his home life was stricken, his school life at Clarke's School in Enfield in Middlesex was full and happy. Here he received a vigorous grammar school education in the reasonably humane atmosphere of a school with a modest library and intelligent if limited masters. Here Keats made one of the great friendships of his life with Charles Cowden Clarke, the son of the headmaster, with whom, after he had left school, Keats used to read Spenser's *The Faerie Queene* in the school grounds to the sound of nightingales in May. He appears to have been a popular, tough, games-loving, active, rather truculent small boy. Towards the end of his school-days he concentrated very much more firmly and enthusiastically on his books. Noted at one time for his indifference to lessons, he became at the end of his school-days an impassioned and prize-winning student.

The death of his mother, the appointment at the instance of his grandmother Mrs Jennings of guardians and trustees for the family, Richard Abbey and John Sandall (effectively the mean-spirited Abbey, whom Keats never got on with, since Sandall took no active part in the duties), and the removal in the summer of John and George from school by Abbey, the one to train as an apothecary – an avocation one stride above a barber, one below a physician – the other to work in Abbey's counting house, will further have diminished the dwindling set of Keats's certainties about life. These events would also have brought home to him the quick of the experience suffered by children whose families are broken by death and disaster, the acrid lessons formulated by a contemporary poet as 'never feel safe now'.[8] We do not know how Keats felt about his removal or his new career. However, he must have applied himself with sufficient degree of application and steadiness to his studies to qualify, which he did by combining his five-year apprenticeship with Thomas Hammond, Surgeon and Apothecary, with a course of study at Guy's Hospital, which he began on 1 October 1815. On 3 March 1816 he registered as a dresser, which suggests, says Robert Gittings, that he intended to prepare for membership of the Royal College of Surgeons. On 25 July 1816 he passed his examinations of the Apothecaries' Hall which qualified him to practise as an apothecary, physician or surgeon. He did this at a time when the examinations had been made stiffer and the licensing of medical people distinctly more professional. In fact he never practised.

Clearly this was a decision, not simply an event. It may have become conscious during the holiday Keats took after his examinations with his brother Tom at Margate. But it must have been working away in his mind during the latter part of his medical training. Keats's reckless decision was a scandal to his cautious guardian but once he made his decision he kept to it. He makes very few explicit references to his medical life and while he may have entertained as a last resort the possibility of restarting it, he only once came near considering it, namely during a week in June 1819 when he wrote gloomily to Dilke: 'I have my choice of three things – or at least two – South America or Surgeon to an I[n]diaman – which last I think will be my fate.'[9] When the grandmother died on 19 December 1814, the first year in which we have evidence of Keats's beginnings as a poet, the last links with the family outside his immediate brothers and sister were snapped. Keats was driven in upon himself – not that his admirable independence would suffer in any way from that – upon his powerful attachment to George and Tom, and his wished-for attachment to Fanny, and finally to the friends he had so fine a faculty for making. These early poems, 'Imitation of Spenser', 'To Byron', 'Fill for me a brimming bowl', 'On Death' and the verse epistle 'To my Brother George', are the first signals of his intention to become a poet, and in much the same category is his verse epistle 'To George Felton Mathew' which was written in November 1815, a month after he had entered Guy's Hospital. His first published poem, 'O Solitude', was printed in the *Examiner* for 5 May 1816, a couple of months before he passed his final examinations. It was in the same year that he first came into touch with Leigh Hunt, Benjamin Robert Haydon and John Hamilton Reynolds, all of whom were to be influential in his life. These and similar friendships, particularly with his old school fellow Charles Cowden Clarke, Richard Woodhouse (another victim of tuberculosis), William Haslam (another school friend), Charles Brown, Joseph Severn, who was with him when he died, James Rice, and Charles and Maria Dilke, who offered him the freedom of their relaxed and affectionate household: these were to substitute in Keats's experience for the higher education he was deprived of. These friendships extended the context in which he lived, offered him occasions for greater experience of the world, of men, and affairs, introduced him to social and literary life, made him acquainted with some of the great figures of the time, with Wordsworth and Shelley, for example, the first of whom he worshipped as a great poet in spite of his intolerable self-centredness, and the second of whom he did not get along with at all. Leigh Hunt at first enraptured Keats; he encouraged him, he printed his poems, and looked upon him as his protégé. Hunt wrote a sweetly insipid verse, whose commonplace thinness and sentimentality, much thought of at the time, Keats came to detest. But Hunt was a generous man, however absurd and eventually maddening his patronizing and proprietorial tone with Keats was. At the beginning of their friendship, his radical stance and anti-establishment politics appealed very much to Keats; two years later Keats found him to be vain and egotistical. But with characteristic generosity, Keats declared two years later again how very much attached he felt he still was to Hunt. Benjamin Haydon, an overpowering, active and disturbing influence, whose tragedy was to think he was a great painter, included Keats's head in a huge *Christ's Entry into Jerusalem*. He was burly, intolerant and vain, but gifted at least in discerning in Keats very early on the lineaments of greatness. Haydon's life eventually collapsed in misery and he committed suicide in 1846. The admirable Charles Wentworth Dilke and his charming wife Maria were faithful friends of Keats and of his family after his death. He was a cultivated civil servant with literary interests who worked in the Navy Pay Office. Keats had a great affection for both of them. Benjamin Bailey was important in Keats's life in that he invited him to spend September 1817 in Oxford with him at Magdalen Hall, where Keats wrote Book III of *Endymion*. Charles Brown was the friend with whom Keats made his tour of England, Scotland and Ireland in the summer of 1818. Keats lived with him after the death of his brother Tom, and in his own illness in 1820 Brown nursed him devotedly. Keats wanted Brown to accompany him to Italy, and when this arrangement proved abortive, it was his painter friend Joseph Severn who went with him. Perhaps the friend who was closest of all to Keats was John Hamilton Reynolds, whom Keats met at Leigh Hunt's house. He was the recipient of some of Keats's most marvellous letters. For Reynolds Keats 'had the greatest power of poetry in him, of any one since Shakespeare'.[10] Reynolds was an amusing, witty man, but also sensible and sympathetic. Keats was very fond of him.

Keats's capacity for friendship, both to provoke it and return it, had to do not only with the generosity of his friends but with the constitution of his own nature. This showed itself in an extraordinary power to discern and imaginatively to become what was particular, unique even, in other forms of life. If he was in the line of those from Dryden to Hopkins able to release and control the energy of the language, he was also, again like Hopkins, of those who used this energy to reveal difference, oddity, the power of a thing to be itself. It was discrete objects – each glitter on each wave – which blazed for Hopkins with a strange individuality. For Keats it was a complex of events, felt to be one structure, but also suddenly seen as having an utter and fundamental singularity. The vivacity, the force of Keats's verbs, belonged to him as one of those able to unleash the activity of the language, but it was also a means perfectly adapted to press out the unique being, the proper quality, of each event.

Keats's experience of the particular fed and sustained his poetic power. In a letter to Thomas Keats which describes a scene in the Lake District and which vividly produces the peculiar character of the place, Keats voices this very sentiment. In the same letter he uses an odd phrase, 'the intellect, the countenance', which carries the same meaning as Hopkins's 'inscape':

What astonishes me more than any thing is the tone, the coloring, the slate, the stone, the moss, the rock-weed; or, if I may so say, the intellect, the countenance of such places. The space, the magnitude of mountains and waterfalls are well imagined before one sees them, but this countenance or intellectual tone must surpass every imagination and defy any remembrance. I shall learn poetry here. . . .[11]

The attraction that 'this countenance or intellectual tone' held for Keats meant that he had an acute susceptibility for forms, for the particular self and structure of a thing, even when it was, in his own words, 'smothered with accidents'. This is a habit of mind or rather a specialization of insight often accompanied, as in many of the poems of Marvell or Hopkins, by an unusual intensity of feeling and a concomitant concentration of expression. Keats certainly believed in the theory that the excellence of an art lay in its intensity. But the qualities of intensity and concentration showed themselves only in the best of his poems since there was, as we shall see, another part of his nature which was infatuated by the drowsily vague and the languorously narcotic, which dimmed his clear eye for the object and betrayed him into the cult of 'silken phrases and silver sentences'. Indeed, Keats's career could be read as the history of the friction of these two elements in his nature.

But so vivid and so strong was this sense of the identity of others in his personal life, so intrusive his images of others that, he reported to Richard Woodhouse, 'When I am in a room with People if I ever am free from speculating on creations of my own brain, then not myself goes home to myself: but the identify of every one in the room begins to press upon me that, I am in a very little time annihilated.'[12] Once, describing the spectacle of a bear-baiting, Keats began irresistibly to imitate the bear:

. . . his legs and arms bent and shortened till he looked like Bruin on his hind legs, dabbing his fore paws hither and thither, as the dogs snapped at him, and now and then acting the gasp of one that had been suddenly caught and hugged – his own capacious mouth adding force to the personation.[13]

And even when he was nursing his beloved brother Tom, so overwhelming was the impression of Tom's identity pressing in upon him that he had to leave the house to be free of it. Nor was his plasticity limited to the influence of human beings: 'if a sparrow come before my window I take part in its existence and pick about the gravel' and 'I lay awake last night – listening to the Rain with a sense of being drown'd and rotted like a grain of wheat'.[14] Or again he was, as he said, entertained – 'entertained' carries the sense of an active becoming as well as the notion of amusement – 'with the alertness of a Stoat or the anxiety of a Deer'. And Severn vividly remembered his capacity to enter into the very being of other things:

> Nothing seemed to escape him, the song of a bird and the undernote of response from covert or hedge, the rustle of some animal, the changing of the green and brown lights and furtive shadows, the motions of the wind – just how it took certain tall flowers and plants – and the wayfaring of the clouds: even the features and gestures of passing tramps, the colour of one woman's hair, the smile on one child's face, the furtive animalism below the deceptive humanity in many of the vagrants, even the hats, clothes, shoes, wherever these conveyed the remotest hint as to the real self of the wearer.[15]

We should err, however, if we supposed that Keats's extraordinary receptiveness to the identity of other things and persons was a mere quirk of temperament or an odd psychological idiosyncrasy. We should be as wrong to think of him as having an unduly passive or feminine nature, or the opposite of what Coleridge saw in Wordsworth, a nature with nothing feminine in it at all. On the contrary his mind had, it seemed to Hopkins, 'the distinctly masculine powers in abundance, his character the manly virtues; but while he gave himself up to dreaming and self-indulgence, of course they were in abeyance'. And we know what Matthew Arnold meant when he said in his indispensable essay, 'the thing to be seized is, that Keats had flint and iron in him, that he had character'.

His outward character as poet, or his public vocation as poet, had been officially inaugurated when in May 1816 Leigh Hunt printed Keats's first published poem in his weekly, the *Examiner*. In August, after he had taken the examinations at Apothecaries' Hall which made him eligible to practise medicine, he went with his sickly brother Tom to Margate from where he addressed a lively letter in verse to his brother George and a similar epistle to his friend Clarke. When he returned from Margate in September the brothers took lodgings together at

8 Dean Street, Southwark. In November they moved to lodgings in Cheapside, and during the same month his sonnet 'On First Looking into Chapman's Homer' was referred to favourably by Hunt, in the first public reference about Keats's work in a critical piece on contemporary young poets which Hunt published in the *Examiner*. During the rest of this year and the beginning of 1817 he was composing verse for a first volume. His friendships with Hunt and Haydon and the Shelleys developed. Haydon, whose propaganding on behalf of the Elgin Marbles was a greater service to art than his painting, took Keats to see them on either 1 or 2 March, a visit which was the occasion for two sonnets on the Marbles. Later in March the brothers moved to Hampstead, to 1 Well Walk, a house which belonged to Benjamin Bentley. At the beginning of March the seal on his poetic profession was set when his first volume of poems was published by C. and J. Ollier. (I shall return to this book in due course.)

This first production fell horribly flat. It was hardly noticed by reviewers. 'Alas!' Clarke remembered many years later, 'the book might have emerged in Timbuctoo with far stronger chance of fame and approbation. It never passed to a second edition; the first was but a small one, and that was never sold off. The whole community, as if by compact, seemed determined to know nothing about it.' James Ollier, one of the two publishing brothers, wrote angrily in answer to some rebuke from George Keats:

> Sir, – We regret that your brother ever requested us to publish his book, or that our opinion of its talent should have led us to acquiesce in undertaking it. We are, however, much obliged to you for relieving us from the unpleasant necessity of declining any further connexion with it, which we must have done, as we think the curiosity is satisfied, and the sale has dropped. By far the greater number of persons who have purchased it from us have found fault with it in such plain terms, that we have in many cases offered to take the book back rather than be annoyed with the ridicule which has, time after time, been showered upon it. . . .[16]

A copy was sent to Wordsworth through the good offices of Haydon and was discovered after Wordsworth's death with most of the pages uncut. Keats himself remarked that the book 'was read by some dozen of my friends who liked it; and some dozen whom I was unaquainted with, who did not'. Hunt neglected to write about it as he

had undertaken to do, and the only strongly favourable review came from Reynolds. Within a month after its appearance Keats was in touch with Reynolds's publishers, John Taylor and James Hessey, who were to prove an altogether more sympathetic firm.

Notes

1 George Santayana, *The Life of Reason*, vol. IV (New York: Charles Scribner's Sons, 1905), p. 194.
2 R. J. White, *Life in Regency England* (London: Batsford, 1963).
3 F. R. and Q. D. Leavis, *Dickens the Novelist* (London: Chatto, 1970), preface, p. xiv.
4 *Inquiring Spirit*, ed. Kathleen Coburn (London: Routledge & Kegan Paul, 1951), p. 317.
5 ibid., p. 351.
6 *The Letters of John Keats: 1814–1821*, ed. Hyder Edward Rollins, 2 vols (Cambridge, Mass.: Harvard University Press, 1958), vol. I, p. 142. (Henceforth cited as *Letters*.)
7 ibid., vol. II, p. 123.
8 D. J. Enright, 'First Death'.
9 *Letters*, II, p. 114.
10 *The Keats Circle*, ed. H. E. Rollins (Cambridge, Mass.: Harvard University Press, 1948), vol. II, p. 173.
11 *Letters*, I, p. 301.
12 ibid., I, p. 387.
13 Walter Jackson Bate, *John Keats* (Cambridge, Mass.: Harvard University Press, and London: Oxford University Press, 1964), p. 117.
14 *Letters*, I, p. 273.
15 William Sharp, *Life and Letters of Joseph Severn* (London: Sampson Low & Co., 1892), p. 19.
16 Bate, op. cit., pp. 150–1.

2
'Poems'

Keats's decision to make himself a poet – because that is what in his mind it came to – was initiated in his later school days when the truculent idler was transformed into the passionate student, and consummated at the conclusion of his medical training. Once taken, the decision was deep and resolute and remained so in spite of a fleeting and near-despairing wavering in January 1819 when he considered the idea of returning to medicine as a ship's surgeon. Becoming a poet, achieving the experienced innocence, the impersonal serenity of the artist, was something Keats had to struggle towards painfully and through successive renunciation. Keats began his poetic life with a corrupted sensibility. The career of many artists moves from simplicity to complexity, or from uncertainty to assurance, or from illusion to reality. The direction of Keats's progress, in ironic contrast to his body, was from sickness to health. We think of corruption as a state supervening on a period of health, or of decadence as the aftermath of vigour; but for the artist himself it can be corruption which comes first and health which has to be striven for. Sensibility itself, a mode of perceiving, ordering, valuing and realizing experience, is far from being wholly within the control of the individual. It is very much an effect of collaboration between the living and the dead. It is largely inherited from tradition, remote and immediate, and it is modified, not only by personal effort, but by family, formal education, and contemporaries. When, as with Keats, tradition was in decline, family sympathetic but in this respect ineffective, contemporaries uncomprehending, it required gifts of genius and heroism of character as well as perseverance beyond the ordinary, to arrive at that health and order which other poets in more fortunate times have started from. The first works of a young poet are more frequently the expression of the will to be a poet than exercises of a poet's powers. They are also, almost necessarily, derivative. And they exhibit, often with pitiless clarity, the modes of sensibility current at the time.

There are some thirty poems in Keats's first volume, and most of them demonstrate the truth of these comments. Why Keats chose these particular poems and put them in the given order has puzzled editors and others. 'It is difficult to understand what principle guided Keats in their selection,' says Ernest de Selincourt.[1] No doubt one was what Keats had to hand that was at least publishable; and another, as W. J. Bate suggests, was 'to put the earliest and poorest poems first . . . [to] allow the reader to feel a progressive rise'.[2] (It is true, though, that the first poem is by no means the weakest in the book.) As to a more internal principle, Jack Stillinger, coolest and most helpful of Keatsian scholars as his compatriate W. J. Bate is the most mellow and sympathetic of biographers, suggests the poems are unified and fall into 'an order determined by Keats's preoccupation with poetry itself and more specifically with the personal question as to whether or not he might become a poet himself'.[3] There is much in Stillinger's idea even if its detailed application fails to grip as closely or explain as fully as he believes. It was to be expected in an increasingly self-conscious age that Keats should be faced by the problem of the very nature of poetry itself, and natural for someone of Keats's background and training to question, as, say, Burns would not have done, his own fitness and willingness to be a poet.

To be a poet: that aspiration, part impulse, part intention, part drowsed desire, informs and shades Keats's beginning. Poetry is a state – at this point even more a state than an activity – and the poet one who exists in that state, and is much less one who engages in the activity. The state is characterized by pleasure – that seems the word rather than happiness – which blends heightened and tingling sense-experience with sensual and vaguely sexual relaxation. In the couplet in 'I Stood Tip-Toe Upon a Little Hill',

> So I straightway began to pluck a posy
> Of luxuries bright, milky, soft and rosy,

'straightway', 'pluck' and 'bright' imply the sharpening of the senses, 'luxuries', 'milky, soft and rosy' the pillowy languor. Intrinsic to this blended state as experienced by the poet – himself almost a passive Lockean recording instrument – is a strain of regret. 'Glory and loveliness have passed away' as it says in the first line of the 'Dedication to

Leigh Hunt Esq.'. The withdrawal is figured in the vanished classical world, drawn from Keats's standby from boyhood, Lemprière's *Classical Dictionary* and Poussin's Arcadian paintings, the references to which are made with nostalgic tenderness as though they were memories of a happy childhood. No 'wreathed incense', no 'crowd of nymphs' now; only 'sweet desolation – balmy pain'. The activity of poetry when it comes into play is aimed at recovering this 'world of blisses'. It is to do so by means of a Wordsworthian relationship with nature. The poet is to join with nature in rebuttal of the urbane values of the eighteenth-century world. But it is a softened Wordsworth, a Wordsworth in velvet, just as the landscape is imagined, arranged, painted. (Titian and Rembrandt, and even more Claude and Poussin, were among the influences who helped to give shape and tone to Keats's sensibility, as Ian Jack pointed out in his commentary on the first book of *Endymion*.[4]) Indeed, the classical figures, pining Narcissus, trembling Syrinx, Arcadian Pan – the epithets tend to be feebly conventional – who were meant to represent and mediate natural forces, are themselves so vague and literary as to be exhalations rather than presences and to swathe with mist the actual scene.

But the Keats one thinks one has netted immediately vaults out. In this poem, by no means the weakest in the book, one sees, in spite of the general impression of derivative second-rateness, there are intimations of another poet. Amid this cluster of shadows and influences which make the conventional, contemporary Keats, there is the intrusion here and there of another, the personal Keats. It comes in an invigorating contrast between two moods: on the one side, 'the languid sick' and their 'fever'd sleep', in a strikingly summoned atmosphere of hectic illness, a sense of which must come from Keats's medical education and family experience, and on the other, the freshness, the coolness of health. There is a wholeness and sanity, as well as a sharpness and actuality in the passages registering this latter mood, which promise a different kind of poetry and which hint at the unique Keatsian grasp of physical reality:

> How silent comes the water round that bend;
> Not the minutest whisper does it send
> To the o'erhanging sallows: blades of grass
> Slowly across the chequered shadows pass –
> Why, you might read two sonnets, ere they reach

To where the hurrying freshnesses aye preach
A natural sermon o'er their pebbly beds;
Where swarms of minnows show their little heads,
Staying their wavy bodies 'gainst the streams,
To taste the luxury of sunny beams
Tempered with coolness. How they ever wrestle
With their own sweet delight, and ever nestle
Their silver bellies on the pebbly sand.

'I Stood Tip-Toe Upon a Little Hill', the first, connects with 'Sleep and Poetry', the last poem in the book. Sleep for Keats seemed to be as significant as dreams for Coleridge, and the half-conscious lapsing into sleep, significant for both. Keats seemed to have thought of sleep as a species of trance, one form of mental intensity, and as an ante-room and analogue of death, the final seal of intensity. In 'Sleep and Poetry', which works more loosely and deliberately with the themes of the earlier poem, we see Keats attempting to order his experience under the banner of a great idea, and providing an inferior form of Wordsworthian philosophic poem:

though no great ministering reason sorts
Out the dark mysteries of human souls
To clear conceiving – yet there ever rolls
A vast idea before me, and I glean
Therefrom my liberty;

But as this poem shows only too clearly, the proper poetic relation of sensation and thought is not achieved by mulling over specific sensations in the light of a vast idea. A relationship more intimate and more informing is required, in which sensation and thought are not divided by the discrepancy implied in Keats's lines. The feebly intellectualized argument of 'Sleep and Poetry' is at points creatively disturbed by suggestions of the true Keats; the indolence gives way to a more keenly apprehensive grasp, and a firmer rhythm and more particularized imagery show a more biting sense of reality:

A pigeon tumbling in clear summer air;
A laughing school-boy, without grief or care,
Riding the springy branches of an elm.

Many critics have attempted to define the character of the two Keatses.

Arnold divides the man with flint and iron in him from the merely sensual one. He uses the indignant distinction made by George Keats between John and Johnny Keats: John had character and was a man of intellectual and spiritual passion; Johnny was the figure invented by Byron, 'that imagined sensuous weakling, the delight of the literary circles of Hampstead'.[5] 'John was the very soul of manliness and courage, and as much like the Holy Ghost as *Johnny Keats*.'[6] Leavis remarks that it seems as if the genius of a major poet were working in the material of minor poetry.

The most recent and, for my purposes, most cogent discrimination, is given by that intense Keatsian critic John Jones. He distinguishes between the romantic Keats and the unique Keats.[7] His initiating insight is located in some lines he quotes from 'In drear-nighted December', a poem written a year after the first book but not published till 1829:

> Ah! would 'twere so with many
>   A gentle girl and boy!
> But were there ever any
>   Writhed not of passèd joy?
> The feel of not to feel it,
> When there is none to heal it,
> Nor numbèd sense to steel it,
> Was never said in rhyme.

'The feel of not to feel it.' The admirably honest Richard Woodhouse who provided three transcripts of these lines confessed an utter abhorrence of the word 'feel' for feeling. 'But', he acknowledged gloomily, 'Keats seems fond of it and will ingraft it (in aeternum) on our language. Be it so.' Garrod, John Jones recalls, changed this line to 'to know the change and feel it' in the face both of the Woodhouse evidence and of Keats's own autograph, showing thereby how difficult it was, even for a scholar like Garrod, not to impose a more general Romantic interpretation on Keats's immediacy of sense.

The substance of John Jones's intuition lies in the difference between feel and feeling. 'Feeling' is Romantic, 'feel' is Keatsian. 'Feeling' drags in its train a what or how or why, an intellectual charge or an explanatory possibility: but the Keatsian 'feel' is pure, sensational, contained, an absolute sense of what is, whether it is space, taste, touch, pressure, temperature or whatever.

> When Keats talks about the feel of solitude or of Shakespeare, he conveys to us no insights into those promising subjects: all truth is contained in, and all attention bent upon, the feel he has of them.[8]

The result is again and again 'that wrapping up of sense' which is in John Jones's view the essence of the Keatsian achievement and what Keats himself was pointing to in another phrase from the famous Teignmouth letter, which is the starting-point of John Jones's inquiry, that 'trembling, delicate and snail-horn perception of beauty'. Paradoxically enough, when one considers the modern psychological usage of the term, the 'perception' involved in this phrase is that purity of sensation, close, end-stopped, unalloyed with any distorting conception, and totally free of anything intellectually *a priori* or consequential, which is what Keats so often and mysteriously succeeds in communicating.

Between 'I Stood Tip-Toe Upon a Little Hill', the vague sketch for a possible longer poem, and 'Sleep and Poetry', the mistier realization of the design, come some five-finger exercises in eighteenth-century Spenser, some arch occasional poems to women, looking sideways to Tom Moore or forward to Swinburne, three verse-letters, two to friends and one to his brother George, and a set of sonnets of which but two are fully achieved, although truly Keatsian lines are scattered over some of the others. Hardly anything available to Keats at the time not in *Poems* deserves to be, except the sonnets 'Written on a Blank Space at the End of Chaucer's Tale of *The Floure and the Leafe*' and 'On Seeing the Elgin Marbles'.

Keats's poems on women show him at his most unattractive, blending Regency masculinity, schoolboy carnality, and Victorian sloppiness. Woman appears as a creamy, sometimes melting, sometimes sulky object. At other times she seems a character in some eighteenth-century pastiche, or again, as in some Victorian novel, a subdued partner in some vaguely incestuous relationship. Arnold, again, refers to the opinion Keats formed of 'the generality of women, who appear to me as children to whom I would rather give a sugar-plum than my time', and to 'a tendency to class women in my books with roses and sweetmeats – they never see themselves dominant'.[9] One discerning critic, however, Christopher Ricks,[10] has even made a case for taking this luscious element in Keats, with that sugar-plum sense of sex which is so pervasively present both in *Poems* and *Endymion*, as inseparable from his seriousness, and a preoccupation with embarrassment as inextricably connected with his most profound moral concerns. Ricks's view, then, is that this ambivalence of feeling is characteristic of Keats's truest imagination. His case is persuasive but, I believe, ultimately unconvincing. Ricks takes as the constituent and moving force of Keats's nature what I judge to be, from the evidence of the letters and the Odes particularly, a distortion, consequent upon deficient early education, contemporary taste, inexperience, the bias of a sensuous nature, and the wretchedness of personal history. Strong as the evidence is for Ricks's Keats, it cannot displace that for an altogether richer, more balanced, more complex and powerful nature.

Perhaps the first stanza of 'Woman! when I behold thee flippant, vain' will sufficiently convey the off-putting flavour of the lesser and superficial Keats:

> Woman! when I behold thee flippant, vain,
>   Inconstant, childish, proud, and full of fancies;
>   Without that modest softening that enhances
> The downcast eye, repentant of the pain
> That its mild light creates to heal again:
>   E'en then, elate, my spirit leaps, and prances,
>   E'en then my soul with exultation dances
> For that to love, so long, I've dormant lain:
> But when I see thee meek, and kind, and tender,
>   Heavens! how desperately do I adore
> Thy winning graces; – to be thy defender
>   I hotly burn – to be a Calidore –
> A very Red Cross Knight – a stout Leander –
>   Might I be loved by thee like these of yore.

These clumsy and frantic posturings which, we are told by Colvin, reduced Keats to tears when he read them over, go oddly with the influence of Spenser to which Keats was introduced by Cowden Clarke. The freshness, pageantry and myth of Spenser appealed strongly to the conventional romantic and the anti-Augustan in Keats, although by an ironic absurdity it was Spenser, as modified by the eighteenth century, by Thomson and Beattie, that Keats was indebted to and most affected by. The tart delineation which Keats gives of the rhythm of eighteenth-century poetry in a passage in 'Sleep and Poetry':

> They sway'd about upon a rocking horse,
> And thought it Pegasus

applies much more markedly to the shapeless couplets of his own two Spenserian pieces, 'Specimen of an Induction to a Poem', and 'Calidore'. But even here, in 'Calidore', among the washed-out artifice and the pre-Raphaelite promise, there is a snatch of more genuine Keats and a touch of the authentic actuality of registration, the 'countenance or intellectual tone' of a place, as he called it, which marks the other Keats:

> Green tufted islands casting their soft shades
> Across the lake; sequester'd leafy glades,
> That through the dimness of their twilight show
> Large dock leaves, spiral foxgloves, or the glow
> Of the wild cat's eyes, or the silvery stems
> Of delicate birch-trees, or long grass which hems
> A little brook.

(The same could not be said of Keats's poem 'Imitation of Spenser', written in 1814, published in 1817, in which the landscape is a purely literary one and in which echoes of Tasso, Milton and Beattie fit neatly together with Spenser in what is technically a very skilful piece of poetic mimicry. Keats himself, one remembers, had a name among his friends since schooldays as a mimic.)

Spenser figures both as an influence and a reference in the three verse-epistles in *Poems*. The first was written during November 1815 to George Felton Mathew to whom the generous Keats attributed, rather in the way that Coleridge did to Bowles, poetic gifts that nobody else could discern. The second, to his brother George, and the third, to Charles Cowden Clarke, the son of Keats's headmaster at Enfield, a good friend and a vigorous stimulus to Keats's literary, musical and political interests, were written at Margate during the summer of 1816, where Keats was on holiday after taking his examinations at the Apothecaries' Hall. (He needed legally to wait till he was twenty-one on 31 October before he could practise.) The tone of the epistles is less hectic and the letter form allows Keats to relax into something closer to the personality he shows in his prose letters. The argument in none of them is close or well knit, and one can hardly speak of anything so complex as an organization in these epistles. A generalization, a memory, an introductory concept, is followed by a catalogue of more or less pertinent examples. But at least each has as a loose theme the real question of poetry as a possible career for Keats. There are the conventional literary and classical references; conventionally favoured writers, Spenser, Shakespeare, Burns, Chatterton; and an odd selection of political heroes, Alfred, Tell, William Wallace and Hunt. But the real life of the epistles occurs among the examples, in the sudden summoning of a living scene, 'a swan superbly frowning', or 'morning shadows streaking into slimness / Across the lawny fields and pebbly waters', or

> The stalks and blades.
> Chequer my tablet with their quivering shades.
> On one side is a field of drooping oats,
> Through which the poppies show their scarlet coats,
> So pert and useless, that they bring to mind
> The scarlet coats that pester human-kind.

The unpretentious gait and simplicity of these last lines from the epistle 'To My Brother George' show the character of Keats forming and hardening amid the literary shadows. The epistles, too, provide Keats with the opportunity for developing an impressive naturalness in the handling of verse, an unforced casualness and ease. The unexpressed premise of many of the poems in *Poems*, that poetry is a drug, a refined form of intoxication, is less languorously apparent in the epistles, where the indolence gives way on occasion to a more energetic and more keenly apprehensive air. At moments the rhythm is firmer, the imagery more particularized, and the language at once more strenuous and more controlled. The epistles, as Stillinger notes,[11] in spite of Keats's optimistic epigraph, disclose misgiving rather than hope about their central preoccupation, namely whether or not Keats could become a poet. If he finds himself so powerless when writing, perhaps he might be more useful to the world in a different vocation.

> Whene'er I venture on the stream of rhyme;
> With shattered boat, oar snapt, and canvas rent
> I slowly sail, scarce knowing my intent.

But all this, and particularly the clarification of intent, points to a development of personality and a movement towards maturity in the poet, since it suggests that he is beginning to grapple with a real problem instead of musing over a classically or medievally insulated predicament. And it means that this growth is taking place in the poet and the poetry as well as in the man and in his letters, although it is more lucid and more secure in the latter.

The set of sonnets included in *Poems* is remarkable on two scores, first for the extraordinary range of quality covered, and second, for the power and perfection of at least one, 'On First Looking into Chapman's "Homer"'. There is a judgement by Coleridge on his own early poems which seems distinctly appropriate to these. While 'such Verses as *strivings* of mind and struggles after the Intense and Vivid are a fair promise of better things', they still are no more than a '*Putting of Thought into Verse*'.[12] 'Putting of Thought into Verse' implies both the duality of the elements out of which the verse is made, namely thought and language, *and* the discrepancy, the gap, which remains when one is put into the other. As the poet grows, the gap closes. The thought is *in* the language, the language is *of* the thought. Some of the thought put into these sonnets is of a sturdily simple, political sort, mixing a sensible patriotism with a decent radicalism. Keats from schooldays had, under the influence of Cowden Clarke, leant very much in this direction. He had read the *Examiner*, Hunt's progressive weekly paper, at school and throughout his life. When Hunt and his brother were imprisoned for a libel on the Prince Regent in 1813, Cowden Clarke brought him presents of fruit and vegetables from the school garden. It was in this context that Keats's acquaintance with Hunt began, and that his natural decency shaped itself towards radical sympathies. But neither in the sonnets printed in *Poems* nor in those written at the same time which were unprinted, did this public and political theme produce that relationship between words and feeling, expression and thought, essential for poetry. Neither in the political poems nor in the sentimental ones to and about women, is there any closure of the gap I spoke of. The relationship between form and feeling is almost the opposite of what Coleridge himself recommended when he wrote: 'The *heart* should have *fed* upon the *truth*, as insects on a leaf, till it be tinged with the colour, and show its food in every the minutest fibre.'[13] There are places in the sonnets, however, in 'To My Brothers', number XVIII, in 'Keen, fitful gusts', number IX, in 'On the Grasshopper and Cricket', number XV, where partially in the first two and completely in the last, theme and language, feeling and form, have the distance between them abolished and each is in and of the other. In two of the sonnets it is only the first third which comes alive in this way. The calm domestic intimacy which starts 'To My Brothers':

> Small, busy flames play through the fresh-laid coals,
> And their faint cracklings o'er our silence creep
> Like whispers of the household gods that keep
> A gentle empire o'er fraternal souls

lapses into something laxer while still inoffensive; in the other one a cold and crackling autumn landscape,

> Keen fitful gusts are whispering here and there
> Among the bushes, half leafless, and dry;
> The stars look very cold about the sky,
> And I have many miles on foot to fare.
> Yet feel I little of the cool bleak air,
> Or of the dead leaves rustling drearily

again becomes mildly sentimental in a Huntian way. Each of the passages I have quoted is notable for its less silken, more abraded surface, for its cooler tone and lower temperature, and this quality of temperate actuality sustains 'On the Grasshopper and Cricket' throughout:

> The poetry of earth is never dead:
> When all the birds are faint with the hot sun,
> And hide in cooling trees, a voice will run
> From hedge to hedge about the new-mown mead –
> That is the Grasshopper's. He takes the lead
> In summer luxury; he has never done
> With his delights, for when tired out with fun
> He rests at ease beneath some pleasant weed.
> The poetry of earth is ceasing never:
> On a lone winter evening, when the frost
> Has wrought a silence, from the stove there shrills
> The Cricket's song, in warmth increasing ever,
> And seems to one in drowsiness half lost,
> The Grasshopper's among some grassy hills.

In this sonnet there is no disproportion, as there is in the ones just quoted, between the different tones and parts of the poem. It operates on one level, or within one sphere of discourse, neither puffing into grandiosity nor sliding into bathos. The opening announcement is saved from any unconfined largeness by the curious collocation of terms: poetry, earth, dead, and by the energizing activity of the phrase 'is never' which works paradoxically to insist on life and movement. It is an example of what Keats was to become a master of, the use of syntax for poetic purposes. Moreover, the generalization which 'The poetry of earth is never dead' constitutes in a formal sense is not simply a category to be succeeded by a catalogue of instances, but rather the precise residue of particular experiences so that the beginning is a distillation evolved from the elements that follow it, and, in spite of its conceptual quality, stands from the beginning with a solidity derived from nature and experience. The body of the piece is composed of a double contrast, first between the birds faint with the hot sun and the thin voice running from hedge to hedge, and secondly between the winter evening and the frost-wrought silence – a delicate Coleridgean effect – and the shrilling activity of the cricket's song, the spare activity of which calls back the grasshopper's in a completed circle of sound. The contrast in each case is between relaxation and energy, between the drowsy warmth of the sun and the stove and the minute vivacity of the cricket's and the grasshopper's voice.

What we have in this sonnet, as in the two passages I quoted just before it, as also in the sonnet 'Written on a Blank Space at the End of Chaucer's Tale of *The Floure and the Leafe*', is a sensibility recalling that of the Shakespeare of *A Midsummer Night's Dream*, lyrical but also exact and steadily and firmly rooted in actuality, and communicating a sense not so much of a vague nature but of the very English countryside. The reader has, to use Keats's phrase, the feel of

dewy drops
Come cool and suddenly against his face,
And by the wandering melody may trace
Which way the tender-leggèd linnet hops.

A more inclusive Shakespearean presence is evident, at least in parts of two sonnets, the one 'On Seeing the Elgin Marbles' (the better of the pair written after seeing the Marbles in company with Haydon, early in March 1817), and the other 'On the Sea'. The first five lines of 'On Seeing the Elgin Marbles' have something of the gulf-enfolding quality of Lear, and they blend together the rounded completion of Shakespearean idiom with that very personal use of the word 'sick':

My spirit is too weak – mortality
  Weighs heavily on me like unwilling sleep,
  And each imagined pinnacle and steep
Of godlike hardship, tells me I must die
Like a sick Eagle looking at the sky.

In the first eight lines of the sonnet 'On the Sea', there is a similar deepening of tone, and of course that lithe energy in the verb which is so characteristically English, Shakespearean and Keatsian:

It keeps eternal whisperings around
  Desolate shores, and with its mighty swell
  Gluts twice ten thousand caverns, till the spell
Of Hecate leaves them their old shadowy sound.
Often 'tis in such gentle temper found,
  That scarcely will the very smallest shell
  Be moved for days from where it sometime fell,
When last the winds of Heaven were unbound.

All these qualities enrich the October 1816 sonnet 'On First Looking into Chapman's "Homer"'. This poem is an integral whole, not a congeries of dissimilar and unequal parts, and the combination of profundity and crispness, of a deep-rolling movement and the finest delicacy of touch rehearse what Keats will be able to do in the Odes.

Much have I travelled in the realms of gold,
  And many goodly states and kingdoms seen;
  Round many western islands have I been
Which bards in fealty to Apollo hold.
Oft of one wide expanse had I been told
  That deep-browed Homer ruled as his demesne;
  Yet did I never breathe its pure serene
Till I heard Chapman speak out loud and bold:
Then felt I like some watcher of the skies
  When a new planet swims into his ken;
Or like stout Cortez when with eagle eyes
  He stared at the Pacific – and all his men
Looked at each other with a wild surmise –
  Silent, upon a peak in Darien.

The simple analogy of reader-traveller is given a broad, shouldering power by Keats's handling and substantiating of the concept of distance, a success to be attributed to his mastery of poetic syntax. The emphasis on 'much' is balanced and strengthened by the physical effort implied in 'round'. To distance he adds as a further instrument the other dimension of time, which again is realized and communicated by the syntactical movements engaged in 'oft', 'yet', 'till' and 'then'. Distance travelled brings us to a particular place and time passed to this moment. The traveller-reader is both the contemplative ('watcher of the skies'), and the creative ('stared at the Pacific') observer. The suspended action, the point in space, the intensity of silence, together compel us into accepting with utter conviction the pure experience of discovery. The effect is produced by the plainest, un-ornamented and even commonplace language. The bards and Apollo, deep-browed Homer and stout Cortez, are no more than conventionally identified. Indeed the poet's use of distance and time requires a certain anonymity in the phrasing, a certain unemphatic quality in the description, since he uses these dimensions as a painter uses light, both as the source of form and the means of movement. Neutrality in the medium suits his purpose in a design which depends so much on pitch, weight, turn, balance, and the steady control of movement.

If in one sense the Chapman Ode is a sport among the other poems in the first book – odd, that is, in being the one, or almost the one poem all of a piece throughout – in another it is representative in collecting and realizing Keatsian powers either smothered or no more than hinted at elsewhere. It is representative in being unromantically, unsubjectively preoccupied in the Shelleyan manner, and representatively Romantic in that Keats is thrilled at resurrecting a neglected element in the poetic tradition. The sonnet's and Keats's connection with the tradition is given by subtleties of management of syntax and rhythm, and by a sustained and buoyant exposition of the argument, a strong and living quality – that of an event taking place at this moment – which brings the whole experience up to the instantaneous present. One sees another form of this intensely active 'nowness' in several of the passages quoted in the last few pages. Keats evokes in these the natural world in process. (And it is the natural world not a mystical or Wordsworthian influence.) The verbs are continuous; there is a sense of stirring molecular activity implicit in the landscape: 'small, busy flames play', 'keen fitful gusts are whispering', 'the poetry of earth is never dead', 'dewy drops come cool and suddenly', the sea

> . . . keeps eternal whisperings around
> Desolate shores, and with its mighty swell
> Gluts twice ten thousand caverns. . . .

The Shakespearean command of actuality, so patent in this side of Keats, goes, strangely, with a deep pull towards dissolution. It is not simply that these are in straightforward opposition, although there is at a superficial level a tension between the part of Keats addicted to the delicious, to exquisite enjoyment, to silken phrases and the voluptuous vein, and that more altert part shown in the verse of a more biting reality. But at a profound level it seems that the Shakespearean gift for creating the real needed for its completion in Keats, or had to be balanced by, the appetite for death. At one level this latter may simply have been a taste for indolent, self-warming luxury, at another, it had the intensely negative force of a passion for oblivion, an instinct for non-being. Lawrence, with his peculiar sense for a poet's relation with life, puts the matter in his own idiom, '. . . and physical consciousness gives a last song in Burns, then is dead. Wordsworth, Keats, Shelley, the Brontës, all are post-mortem poets. The essential instinctive–intuitive body is dead, and worshipped in death – all very unhealthy.'[14] Keats, as Lawrence said again, 'for ever yearning for something outside himself', also yearned for total dissolution. But even in this he is, according to Lawrence, different from the other Romantics. Keats's fascination with death is expressed in such a way that we feel his engagement: 'Shelley is pure escape: the body is sublimated into sublime gas. Keats is more difficult – the body can still be *felt* dissolving in waves of successive death.'[15]

Two lines, then, according to Lawrence, merge in Keats: on the one hand the post-Elizabethan rupture in human consciousness in which 'the mental consciousness [recoils] in violence away from the physical, instinctive–intuitive;'[16] on the other, his yearning for selflessness, for otherness, becomes that extreme form of otherness, a yearning for non-being.

Notes

1 E. de Selincourt, *The Poems of John Keats* (London: Methuen, 1926), p. 388.
2 Bate, *John Keats*, p. 141.
3 Cf. Jack Stillinger, *The Hoodwinking of Madeline* (Urbana: University of Illinois Press, 1971), p. 5.

4 Ian Jack, *Keats and The Mirror of Art* (Oxford: Clarendon Press, 1967), pp. 149–51.
5 Matthew Arnold, *Essays in Criticism* (London: Macmillan, 1888), p. 112.
6 ibid., p. 106.
7 Cf. John Jones, *John Keats's Dream of Truth* (London: Chatto, 1969), pp. 41–68.
8 ibid., p. 10.
9 Matthew Arnold, op. cit., pp. 114–15.
10 Cf. Christopher Ricks, *Keats and Embarrassment* (Oxford: Clarendon Press, 1974).
11 Stillinger, op. cit., p. 9.
12 *The Poems of Samuel Taylor Coleridge*, ed. Ernest Hartley Coleridge (London: Oxford University Press, 1927), p. 2 n.
13 E. L. Griggs, *Collected Letters of Samuel Taylor Coleridge* (Oxford: Clarendon Press, 1956–9), vol. I, p. 115.
14 *D. H. Lawrence: Selected Literary Criticism*, ed. Anthony Beal (London: Heinemann, 1955), p. 54.
15 ibid., p. 64.
16 ibid., p. 54.

3
'Endymion'

I have commented already on Keats's remarking within himself 'a horrid morbidity of temperament' which made him liable to bouts of extreme tension and to the deepest depression. But this part of his nature was balanced by qualities of sanity and buoyancy which made it possible for him to shrug off blows that might have disabled another, like his first book's total flop. This rational vitality, quickened by humour, spirit, self-mockery and courage, gives strength and appeal to what we have increasingly come to see as Keats's greatest creative achievement after his poetry, his letters, of which some 320 survive. This correspondence was already in full swing when Keats paid his holiday visit in the spring of 1817 to Southampton, the Isle of Wight, and Margate, during which he was planning his second volume of verse, *Endymion*, and beginning to write it after Tom joined him at Margate on 24 April. His letters to his family, easy, intimate, affectionate, are particularly illuminating about his inner life, as indeed are those to his closest friends Clarke and Reynolds. They record and evoke his spiritual and poetic growth; they are an artist's diary, they are workbooks in which he developed his profoundest concerns, the themes of his poetry, and his deepening insight into human life and values. They also strikingly confirm Coleridge's belief that there never was a great poet who did not also possess 'depth and energy of thought'.[1] They are dappled with appealing evidence of his own attractive and maturing personality. Part of that, and a quality contributing markedly to the active buoyancy of his letters, is an incessant fascination with every form of existence, a constant interrogation of life and experience.

> This it is that makes the Amusement of Life – to a speculative Mind. I go among the Fields and catch a glimpse of a stoat or a fieldmouse peeping out of the withered grass – the creature hath

> a purpose and its eyes are bright with it – I go amongst the buildings of a city and I see a Man hurrying along – to what? The Creature has a purpose and his eyes are bright with it.[2]

During this summer Keats continued his studies in Shakespeare, always his comfort and standby. He persevered with *Endymion*, working on it several conscientious hours a day. It would be, he said, 'a test, a trial of my Powers of Imagination and chiefly of my invention which is a rare thing indeed – by which I must make 4000 Lines of one bare circumstance and fill them with Poetry'.[3] He was less susceptible to the influence of Hunt – particularly after he saw Hunt's delayed and patronizing review of his first book, and less dependent on him as his awareness of his own poetic power developed. He put on a youthful, slightly embarrassed version of the professional author's attitude when he applied twice to Taylor and Hessey for advances. There seems to be little doubt that Keats, who had hoped that the girls on the Isle of Wight might turn out to be 'a little profligate', was probably infected during this summer with gonorrhea. In early October he was certainly taking mercury, a well-known contemporary specific. He spent as usual much time and energy on his brothers' problems, on Tom's illness and George's disorderly business career.

From 3 September to 5 October 1817 occurred one of the most relaxed and agreeable episodes in Keats's career. He accepted an invitation from a new friend, Benjamin Bailey, to spend a month in the long vacation with him at Magdalen Hall, Oxford. Bailey was rather older than the usual undergraduate. By this time he was some twenty-five years of age. He became unpopular with some of Keats's friends later because, being clearly of a would-be uxorious bent, he rather clumsily wooed in quick succession several girls, flitting from one to the other like a large bumble bee. But Keats had the highest opinion of him, at least of his character. He was reading for the Church but there was sufficient of the eighteenth century left in Regency clerical students for him to enjoy parties, drink and bawdy. He was also well off. He had not only a profound admiration for Keats but very considerable discernment into his nature and genius. Bailey eventually married Miss Gleig, the daughter of the Bishop of Stirling, and served much of his career abroad, probably because of his wife's ill health, and ended as Archdeacon of Colombo. Richard Monckton Milnes, Keats's first biographer, assumed that Bailey was long dead and had not therefore got in touch with him. When Bailey found this out he wrote from Ceylon what W. J. Bate calls 'one of the three or four most valuable [letters] left by any of Keats's friends'.[4] In the course of it he points out how Keats 'was the most *loveable* creature, in the proper sense of that word, as distinguished from *amiable*, I think I ever knew as a man'.[5] He remarked on Keats's sensitive generosity to others, and he maintained that while Keats's errors of sensibility were to be attributed to his deficiencies in education, he also had within him the instincts of health and growth: 'like the Thames waters, when taken out to sea, he had the rare quality of purifying himself.'[6]

Keats worked hard and regularly at Oxford – writing, with as much regularity and apparently with as much ease, as he wrote his letters – but he also found the company of Bailey, the surroundings, the weather, the entertainment, the boating, and the pleasures of university life, wonderfully reviving. 'This Oxford,' he wrote to his sister Fanny, 'I have no doubt is the finest City in the world – it is full of old Gothic buildings – Spires – towers Quadrangles – Cloisters Groves & is surrounded with more Clear streams than ever I saw together – I take a Walk by the Side of one of them every Evening and thank God, we have not had a drop of rain these many days.'[7] And to the Reynolds sisters: 'here am I among Colleges, Halls Stalls plenty of Trees thank God – plenty of Water thank heaven – plenty of Books thank the Muses – plenty of Snuff – thank Sir Walter Raleigh – plenty of Sagars, ditto – plenty of flat Country – thank Tellus's rolling pin. I'm on the Sofa – Buonapa[r]te is on the Snuff Box.'[8] During this cheerful Oxford time, while persisting with *Endymion*, he continued to enlarge his reading, concentrating on Milton, Dante in Cary's translation, Wordsworth, Hazlitt and the Bible. He came, too, under the influence of Bailey, to develop a less tense and irritable attitude towards religion, and while he certainly never became an active believer, he showed a less exasperated and more mature feeling for the whole subject: 'He was no scoffer, and in no sense was he an infidel,' reported Bailey.

Keats came back to his noisy Hampstead lodgings. His brothers had already returned from their French expedition. He went on trying to raise money for a protégé of Haydon's, a young painter, Charles Cripps. This was a project which went tediously on during the next year. He continued to treat himself with mercury. His literary friends bickered cattily among themselves, and Keats vowed impatiently that he would have nothing more to do with any of them except Wordsworth. *Blackwood's* published its first attack called 'On the Cockney School of Poetry', directed primarily at Hunt. The second, which blasted Keats, was not to appear till August next year. Other reviews of his first volume of poems in the *Monthly Magazine*, the *Scots Magazine*, the *Eclectic Review* and the *European Magazine* were not unappreciative and occasionally perceptive. They were also unlikely to allay Keats's own anxiety about his first production. But more depressing than all was the health of Tom, who was already giving evidence, even if it was not yet recognized, of the family disease. In order to finish *Endymion* Keats visited Burford Bridge near Box Hill, where he read Shakespeare and completed *Endymion* on 28 November, writing something like five hundred lines in six days. As he was inclined to do after a long poem, he composed a short one, in this instance an exquisite one, a signal of completion and relief. I have referred to it before and it is short enough to quote:

In drear-nighted December

I

In drear-nighted December,
Too happy, happy tree,
Thy branches ne'er remember
Their green felicity:
The north cannot undo them,
With a sleety whistle through them,
Nor frozen thawings glue them
From budding at the prime.

II

In drear-nighted December,
Too happy, happy brook,
Thy bubblings ne'er remember
Apollo's summer look;
But with a sweet forgetting,
They stay their crystal fretting,
Never, never petting
About the frozen time.

III
Ah! would 'twere so with many
A gentle girl and boy!
But were there ever any
Writhed not of passèd joy?
The feel of not to feel it,
When there is none to heal it,
Nor numbèd sense to steel it,
Was never said in rhyme.

Keats's own estimation of *Endymion*, delivered in a letter to John Taylor at the end of February, was detached and in proportion. He realized that its importance came from the part it played in his general development, rather than from its intrinsic merit: 'In *Endymion* I have most likely but moved into the Go-cart from the leading strings. . . . If Endymion serves me as a Pioneer perhaps I ought to be content. . . . I am anxious to get Endymion printed that I may forget it and proceed.'[9] Wordsworth, to whom Keats, after the proper approaches were made, was introduced through the good offices of Haydon, is reported in Haydon's *Journals* to have said drily of the 'Hymn to Pan' from *Endymion*, 'a Very pretty piece of Paganism'.[10] According to Haydon, Keats was deeply wounded and never forgave Wordsworth. Gittings writes that this was written nearly thirty years after the event, 'when Haydon's megalomaniac tendencies were tipping over into insanity'.[11] Certainly Keats's letters give no evidence of any unrelenting hostility towards Wordsworth, and as for the remark itself, it seems to me distinctly characteristic of Wordsworth, not wholly unwarranted, and not altogether unkindly in intention. It is of a piece, indeed, with what Wordsworth's sister-in-law Sara Hutchinson remembered as having in mind herself on the same occasion: 'I wonder anybody should take such subjects now-a-days.'[12] It is odd that the second Greek renaissance, in which Greek culture swept across Europe during the eighteenth century, not mediated by Latin as in the first phase, but brought now in its pure Greek form, should have had such an unremarkable influence on the English Romantics, and should be notable only for such minor works as Byron's *Manfred* and Wordsworth's *Laodamia* and Keats's *Endymion* – that gymnastic exercise, as Walter Jackson Bate called it. Undoubtedly its greatest result in English nineteenth-century literature was the 'Ode on a Grecian Urn', that amazingly pure distillation of the

Greek spirit, the poem which makes us realize the truth of Eliot's comment that some men absorb knowledge while others have to sweat for it. But this was an isolated case. Keats scoured the classics because he felt he could find there a subject and a machinery. In fact what he wanted in a much more important sense, as he himself came to realize, was poetic material. His own life and thought were to supply that in an infinitely more influential way than anything he could find in Greek myth.

Reactions to *Endymion* vary from the disgusted to the indifferent, and from the indifferent to the luke-warm. Let me illustrate this with a handful of representative opinions. Lockhart, expressing the last vestiges of Augustan taste, wrote in *Blackwood's Edinburgh Magazine* in August 1818, 'The phrenzy of the *Poems* was bad enough in its way; but it did not alarm us half so seriously as the calm, settled, imperturbable drivelling idiocy of *Endymion*.'[13] The *British Critic* voiced a pre- and near-Victorian view:

> We will not disgust our readers by retailing to them the artifices of vicious refinement, by which, under the semblance of 'slippery blisses, twinkling eyes, soft completion of faces, and smooth excess of hands,' he would palm upon the unsuspicious and the innocent, imaginations better adapted to the stews.[14]

Gerard Manley Hopkins, that unrepresentative Victorian, was more sympathetically discriminating:

> Since I last wrote I have reread Keats a little. . . . He was, in my opinion, made to be a thinker, a critic, as much as a singer or artist of words. This can be seen in certain reflective passages, as the opening to *Endymion* and others in his poems. These passages are the thoughts of a mind very ill instructed and in opposition; keenly sensible of wrongness in things established but unprovided with the principles to correct that by. Both his principles of art and his practice were in many things vicious, but he was correcting them, even eagerly.[15]

George Santayana, the subtlest and wittiest of philosophic critics, remarked of *Endymion*,

> Long passages in Shelley's *Revolt of Islam* and Keats's *Endymion* are poetical in this sense; the reader gathers, probably, no definite

> meaning, but is conscious of a poetic medium, of speech euphonious and measured, and redolent of a kind of objectless passion which is little more than the sensation of the movement and sensuous richness of the lines.[16]

John Jones, in general an ardently sympathetic critic, writes in our day:

> *Endymion* is a rambling storehouse of pleasures, but of pleasures which claim a new gravity by doting on their own fair features and murmuring from time to time, 'Beauty!' This narcissistic exercise does more than anything else to make the poem the airless, eventless, self-caressing thing it so disagreeably is.[17]

Each of these critics makes, I believe, a valid point, but none of them has spoken with more temperate accuracy than Keats himself in his remarkable Preface, the expression of a nature in which there was not a touch of the histrionic, or of what Santayana again called 'romantic ignorance of self', at least until he was in the last stages of sickness.

> Knowing within myself the manner in which this Poem has been produced, it is not without a feeling of regret that I make it public.
>
> What manner I mean, will be quite clear to the reader, who must soon perceive great inexperience, immaturity, and every error denoting a feverish attempt, rather than a deed accomplished. . . .
>
> The imagination of a boy is healthy, and the mature imagination of a man is healthy; but there is a space of life between, in which the soul is in a ferment, the character undecided, the way of life uncertain, the ambition thick-sighted: thence proceeds mawkishness, and all the thousand bitters which those men I speak of must necessarily taste in going over the following pages.

Let me refer for a moment to each of these comments. We can reasonably ignore *Blackwood's* abusive phrase 'drivelling idiocy', though '. . . a bunch of blooming plums / Ready to melt between an infant's gums' is not the only couplet that merits the term. But in using the terms 'calm', 'settled' and 'imperturbable', Lockhart fastens on one of the constitutive weaknesses of *Endymion*, namely that it is, as W. J. Bate says in his illuminating biographical treatment of the poem, an act of the will. It was begun by Keats in a deliberate effort to test his powers and to submit himself to a trial, the trial of length. 'Did our great Poets ever write short Pieces?' he curiously enquires. Keats himself, comically parodying Endymion, speaks of 'my friend Keats', 'hawling me through the Earth and Sea with unrelenting Perseverance'. 'Hawling' Endymion about aptly describes how Keats conducts his passive hero through vast galleries of space, and suggests something of the determination with which he sat down to his table each day to do his necessary quota of lines. It is instructive to compare Keats's long poem with Coleridge's long poem *The Ancient Mariner*. In Keats the activity of the will is in violent contrast to the natural way in which Coleridge's poem evolved. Wordsworth's hint, filled out with Coleridge's own reading in the literature of voyages and of conversion, and touched by the influence of Percy and a medieval religious pattern, offered Coleridge a character, a situation, a drama, a geography and context, a machinery wholly fitted to encourage that combination of management and acceptance necessary in art. The world of *The Ancient Mariner*, so inclusive and so dramatic, powerfully attracted the poet's profoundest experience: it strongly encouraged that essential flow of unconscious forces of which Coleridge said:

> In every work of art there is a reconcilement of the external and the internal, the conscious is so impressed on the unconscious as to appear in it. . . . He who combines the two is the man of genius; and for that reason he must partake of both. Hence there is in genius itself an unconscious activity: nay, that is the genius in the man of genius.

In Keats's case the hint he had taken from his own earlier poem. 'I Stood Tip-Toe Upon a Little Hill', 'the bare circumstance' out of which he was to make four thousand lines and fill them with poetry, pieced out with information from Tooke's *Pantheon* and Lemprière's *Classical Dictionary*, and touched up with some Elizabethan cosmetics, did nothing of the same kind for him. Although he had an intuitive sense of the permanent cogency of Greek myth to human character, its application in the ardently listless *Endymion* provides nothing of the intrinsic drama, setting, and inclusive human significance that Coleridge derived from the sources of *The Ancient Mariner*. In particular, the fable – the mortal's hackneyed search for the divine ultimately found embodied in the human – did not prove capable of provoking that flow of unconscious activity, the genius in Keats's genius. What was unconscious and not at all part of that genius, was the immature and narcissistic sexuality justly pointed out, in however shrill and absurd an idiom, by the *British Critic*.

> Sideway his face reposed
> On one white arm, and tenderly unclosed,
> By tenderest pressure, a faint damask mouth
> To slumbery pout; just as the morning south
> Disparts a dew-lipped rose.

No doubt it was lines of this sort, and others of an even more feverish and swooning ripeness, which Gerard Manley Hopkins had in mind when he spoke of Keats's principles and practice of art being in many things vicious, although it was neither Keats's principles nor his art but rather his instinct, his sensibility, which was vicious, infected, that is, by an infantile seeking and sucking of pleasure. And probably it was the contemplative beginning of Book I Hopkins was thinking of among other things when he detected in Keats capacities as a thinker and a critic. Such capacities Keats certainly possessed, but they had hardly at this stage begun to affect his poetry, although they were already highly developed in his letters, where we feel Keats's grasp and assimilation in the vitality of his independent idiom, in his powerful discernment of totally new connections and in his capacity for creative speculation. Possibly Hopkins was thinking of the enlargement of intention, the Wordsworthian ambition to communicate moral and philosophic truth by means of narrative – surely never as allegory – which Keats certainly had as part of his purpose in this poem. But there is no organic development from the famous 'A thing of beauty is a joy for ever' passage to the rest of the poem. It comes first as a signal of intention, and as far as the development of the poem is concerned, it might as well not be there at all. It seems to me that if we combine Hopkins's discernment of a more complex and telling purpose to the poem, with the actuality registered by Santayana of objectless passion, sensation, movement and sensuous richness devoid of precise meaning, we come closer to recording our reaction to *Endymion*. When Keats spoke of it himself as 'mawkish', he may have been too severe, but not much. The poem is fluent, facile, sweetly insipid. There is no leading idea, and certainly none of any generating power, unless we call Endymion's search for self-fulfilment through beauty and sex one, and little that is remarkable in detail, and that only in passages in which pleasure ceases to be a lolling, subjective indulgence and becomes an element in the more complex experience of the natural world.

We have, then, on the one side the melting ice-cream of lines like 'O he had swooned / Drunken from Pleasure's nipple' or a more sexually squirming passage like the following:

> One morn she left me sleeping: half awake
> I sought for her smooth arms and lips, to slake
> My greedy thirst with nectarous camel-draughts;
> But she was gone.

On the other, an attractively muted Shakespearean echo:

> She sings but to her love, nor e'er conceives
> How tip-toe Night holds back her dark-grey hood,

or the more sense-packed and promising particularity of:

> O thou, to whom
> Broad-leavèd fig trees even now foredoom
> Their ripened fruitage; yellow-girted bees
> Their golden honeycombs; our village leas
> Their fairest-blossomed beans and poppied corn;
> The chuckling linnet its five young unborn
> To sing for thee; low creeping strawberries
> Their summer coolness; pent up butterflies
> Their freckled wings; yea, the fresh budding year
> All its completions – be quickly near,
> By every wind that nods the mountain pine,
> O forester divine!

As for the thought, it seems even more a mirage in *Endymion* than philosophy was an illusion in *The Prelude*. It varies between what John Jones called the hollow spirituality of the Pleasure Thermometer:

> But there are
> Richer entanglements, enthralments far
> More self-destroying, leading, by degrees,
> To the chief intensity: the crown of these
> Is made of love and friendship, and sits high
> Upon the forehead of humanity.
> All its more ponderous and bulky worth

Is friendship, whence there ever issues forth
A steady splendour; but at the tip-top,
There hangs by unseen film, an orbèd drop
Of light, and that is love:

and the cloudy relaxation and the over-stretched speculative vagueness of:

Be still the unimaginable lodge
For solitary thinkings; such as dodge
Conception to the very bourne of heaven,
Then leave the naked brain; be still the leaven
That spreading in this dull and clodded earth
Gives it a touch ethereal – a new birth;

It is, of course, possible to say more in defence, or support, of *Endymion* than that it contains the odd, distributed passage of genuinely accomplished or truly promising Keats – the Keats of the Odes and the revised *Hyperion*. *Endymion* did, in fact, occupy some eight months of Keats's short career and represents a large proportion of the poetry published during his lifetime. Biographical critics, therefore, like Walter Jackson Bate and Aileen Ward in particular, have transferred significance from the poem to the poet. Bate writes, for example,

> The essential, obvious psychological interest of *Endymion* . . . is that we have a manly intelligence, blessed with instinctive prudence as well as a trustful veneration of what the best of the past has achieved, deliberately using these months, using this long worksheet, so to speak, as a courageous exercise, confident that by such a stretch of inventive muscle he was following the examples he revered, and that the principal gain of such an exercise would appear not in the poem itself but in what he would write later – possibly much later.[18]

Aileen Ward, having specified the obvious faults of immaturity in *Endymion*, insists that it is a uniquely interesting work concerned with the central experience of a young man, namely that of erotic love, and claims that Keats discovered the full meaning of what he was writing only as he was writing it. This meaning included first, the power of sexual love utterly to cancel the divisions between the self and the world outside it, and secondly, on the psychological or symbolic level, the realization of the superficiality of Endymion's adolescent dream of 'endless bliss'.

> The ambiguity is inescapable; Keats's legend pulled him in one direction, his experience in another. . . . Through Endymion's adventures Keats attempted to state, however gropingly, his belief in the necessity of growth, the value of the progression into experience, the impossibility of regression into innocence, the goal of a more complex harmony of being.[19]

The first part of Aileen Ward's comment, in which she speaks of the movement in *Endymion* towards a more complex harmony, applies more to Keats's intention, as her phrase 'however gropingly' implies, rather than to anything rendered in the text of the poem. The second part, where she refers to the capacity of sex to obliterate the boundary between self and the world outside, more accurately describes a key element both in *Endymion* and the immature personality of Keats. It is an extension of what I called, when speaking of *Poems*, a passion for oblivion and an instinct for non-being. It is what Lawrence sensed in Keats, even in the Odes. It is the atavistic, the destructive side of the Shakespearean quality of Negative Capability. Whereas Negative Capability, both in Shakespeare and Keats, is, paradoxically given its name, positive and creative, the impulse to dissolve the personality in sex, or the object tasted in taste itself – a characteristic mode of sense-experience in *Endymion* – is a bias leading to the disintegration of immediate existence and a relapse into a more primitive and finally formless state. There are phrases in *Endymion* which make us aware of this effort to escape from what Keats feels to be the cell of self. He speaks in Book II, as though it were an imprisoning discomfort, of 'the journey homeward to habitual self'; and in the same book, of 'The goal of consciousness? Ah, 'tis the thought, / The deadly feel of solitude:' and again in Book II he points to the contrast between conscious existence and dissolution in a way which suggests where his own inclination lies: 'To make us feel existence, and to show / How quiet death is,' something confirmed by and connected with his consistent contrasting of fever and coolness:

> A homeward fever parches up my tongue –
> O let me slake it at the running springs!

Notes

1 Cf. *Biographia Literaria*, XV, ed. J. Shawcross (Oxford: Clarendon Press, 1907).
2 *Letters*, II, pp. 79–80.
3 ibid., I, pp. 169–70.
4 Bate, *John Keats*, p. 197.
5 ibid., pp. 197–8.
6 ibid., p. 198.
7 *Letters*, I, p. 154.
8 ibid., pp. 149–50.
9 ibid., pp. 238–9.
10 Robert Gittings, *John Keats* (London: Heinemann, 1968), p. 167.
11 ibid.
12 *The Letters of Sara Hutchinson, 1800–1835*, ed. Kathleen Coburn (Oxford: Oxford University Press, 1954), p. 133.
13 John Gibson Lockhart, 'The Cockney School of Poetry', *Blackwood's Edinburgh Magazine*, vol. III, no. xvii, August 1818, pp. 519–24.
14 Bate, *John Keats*, p. 370.
15 Gerard Manley Hopkins to Coventry Patmore, 6 May 1888. *The Further Letters of Gerard Manley Hopkins*, ed. Claude Colleer Abbott (London, New York, Toronto: Oxford University Press, 1938).
16 George Santayana, *Interpretations of Poetry and Religion* (New York: Evanston, and London: Harper & Row, 1957), p. 256.
17 Jones, *John Keats's Dream of Truth*, pp. 128–9.
18 Bate, *John Keats*, p. 170.
19 Aileen Ward, 'Endymion' in *Critics on Keats*, ed. Judith O'Neill (London: Allen & Unwin, 1967), pp. 46–7. (From *John Keats: The Making of a Poet* (London: Secker & Warburg, 1963), pp. 141–6.)

4
The developing self

Keats's life was harsh and sad, his thought rich and complex. The grimness of life, experienced from the first in the tragic deaths of his father and his mother, and the shattering of the family, was brought home to him again by the state of Tom's health, which now gave unmistakable signs of consumption. In January he was spitting blood, and another agonizing period in Keats's life, of anxiety and fear, was starting. It is probably hard for anyone brought up in the last twenty years to feel, in the way Keats must have felt, the thrill of horror and doom which the diagnosis of consumption could provoke. It carried with it suggestions of fate, misery and terror. Keats was now, during January and February 1818, seeing his *Endymion* through the press. Earlier in December Haydon had taken Keats's life-mask and painted his head along with Hazlitt's, Wordsworth's and Voltaire's into his enormous canvas *Christ's Entry into Jerusalem*. Tom, who was too ill to stay in London, was taken by George, unemployed at this time, to the milder climate of Teignmouth. Keats was also living, in his characteristically energetic, pleasure-loving and courageous way, a vigorous social life. He saw Wordsworth more than once, attended dances, dined out frequently – one such dinner was at Haydon's, where the guests included Wordsworth and Lamb, and occasionally attended wild parties, often on a Saturday night. He saw his sister several times when she was in London with the Abbeys. He was attending Hazlitt's lectures. Altogether, it is easy to see why he wrote, 'I have been racketing too much and do not feel too well.'

The most powerful and productive influence on Keats's thought, a word I want to use in the largest and most inclusive way, is Shakespeare. He had already outgrown the sentimental tutelage of Hunt; he was of course deeply impressed by Wordsworth, certainly Wordsworth's concept of the moral nature of the poet's function, although their sensibilities were of such totally different kinds that the inflence does not show itself directly in the poetry; he was about to enter the period when he was most actively under the influence of Milton. But the most constant, as the most radical, influence was Shakespeare's, a fact which argues potentialities of greatness in Keats himself. Only someone with something of the Shakespearean quality could absorb and reconstitute as his own so potent a force. A sign of that in his practical, daily life, was the influence of Hazlitt on him, which now replaced that of Hunt. It was the Hazlitt of the essay *On the Principles of Human Action* and the lectures *On the English Poets*. Above all it was Hazlitt's emphasis on intensity in art and his appreciation of the concrete which appealed so much to Keats. Coleridge, who strangely had very little influence on Keats – he certainly knew his work, having read Charles Dilke's copy of *Sybilline Leaves* – devoted his life to displacing Locke's theory of the human mind as 'a lazy looker on at an external universe', in favour of a positive creative concept in which the mind grapples with and shapes its experience. In Locke's theory the subject was passive, the object active. Keats went back to the truth lurking in Locke, which Hazlitt so clearly saw, namely that there was a sense in which the mind had within itself the potentiality of becoming, a quality which required the condition of passivity, or waiting, or being able. Like Coleridge he rejected the mechanistic element in Locke, but he did accept the view of consciousness as process or becoming. A clear demonstration of his debt, to Shakespeare and to Hazlitt, can be seen in the review which he wrote after seeing Edmund Kean in *Richard III* at Drury Lane. His friend John Reynolds asked Keats to take his place as dramatic critic for this and two other pieces:

> Mr Kean's two characters of this week, comprising as they do the utmost of quiet and turbulence, invite us to say a few words on his acting in general. . . . There is an indescribable gusto in his voice, by which we feel that the utterer is thinking of the past and the future, while speaking of the instant. When he says in Othello 'put up your bright swords, for the dew will rust them,' we feel that his throat had commanded where swords were as thick as reeds. From eternal risk, he speaks as though his body were unassailable. Again, his exclamation of 'blood, blood, blood!' is direful and slaughterous to the deepest degree, the very words appear stained and gory. His nature hangs over them, making a

prophetic repast. His voice is loosed on them, like the wild dogs on the savage relics of an eastern conflict; and we can distinctly hear it 'gorging and growling o'er carcase and limb.' In Richard, 'Be stirring with the lark to-morrow, gentle Norfolk!' (*Richard III* v.iii.56) comes from him, as through the morning atmosphere, towards which he yearns. We could cite a volume of such immortal scraps, and dote upon them with our remarks; but as an end must come, we will content ourselves with a single syllable. It is in those lines of impatience to the night who, 'like a foul and ugly witch, doth limp so tediously away' (*Henry V* IV, Chorus 21–2). Surely this intense power of anatomizing the passion of every syllable – of taking to himself the wings of verse, is the mean[s] by which he becomes a storm with such fiery decision; and by which, with a still deeper charm, he 'does his spiriting gently' (*The Tempest* I.ii.298). Other actors are continually thinking of their sum-total effect throughout a play. Kean delivers himself up to the instant feeling, without a shadow of a thought about any thing else. He feels his being as deeply as Wordsworth, or any other of our intellectual monopolists. From all his comrades he stands alone, reminding us of him whom Dante has so finely described in his Hell:

And sole apart retir'd, the Soldan fierce. (*Inferno* IV, 126)[1]

The active receptiveness which Keats notes in Kean, he thinks of as part of the substance of the actor's art; he also thought of it as part of the substance of the poet's art. Keats was later to make an explicit connection between this capacity for sensitive openness and the essential character of the poet after his trip to the Lake District and Scotland in the summer of 1818, a trip made in the hope of getting a closer grasp of the genius of Wordsworth. (He did not meet Wordsworth in the Lake District, and had no chance to change the view he had gained of him in London, where he said Wordsworth had left a bad impression everywhere, by reason of his 'egotism, vanity and bigotry'.)

As to the poetical character itself (I mean that sort of which, if I am any thing I am a Member; that sort distinguished from the Wordsworthian or egotistical sublime; which is a thing per se and stands alone) it is not itself – it has no self – it is every thing and nothing – it has no character – it enjoys light and shade. . . .

> What shocks the virtuous philosop[h]er delights the camelion Poet. . . . A Poet is the most unpoetical of any thing in existence; because he has no Identity.[2]

The poet's anonymity is far from being a mere vacancy, a weakness or a defect. It is the quality which goes 'to form a man of Achievement especially in Literature' and its varying intensity is what distinguishes the greater from the lesser writer. He wrote to his brothers on 21 December 1817, 'I mean *Negative Capability*, that is when man is capable of being in uncertainties, Mysteries, doubts, without any irritable reaching after fact & reason – Coleridge, for instance, would let go by a fine isolated verisimilitude caught from the Penetralium of mystery, from being incapable of remaining content with half knowledge.'[3] Upon the poet so endowed there lay, thought Keats, the duty, almost the moral duty, to be still, to contemplate, to wait upon the event. When he had written the following comment, Keats with characteristically wry and pleasing self-dismissal observed that he might well have been deceived into offering as a general truth what was no more than a sophistical defence of his own indolence. Even so, he believed, his remark was the neighbour to the truth. 'Let us not therefore go hurrying about and collecting honey-bee like, buzzing here and there impatiently from a knowledge of what is to be arrived at: but let us open our leaves like a flower and be passive and receptive.'[4] And elsewhere he wrote: 'The Genius of Poetry must work out its own salvation in a man: It cannot be matured by law & precept, but by sensation & watchfulness in itself – That which is creative must create itself.'[5]

In mentioning Keats's characteristic self-dismissal I am referring incidentally to something, in part a gift of intelligence, in part a disposition of character, which is sufficiently important – in that it brought an added strength to Keats as a poet – to be considered expressly. I mean an unusual degree of self-awareness. To say this is not to impute to Keats a narcissistic self-interest. He does indeed offer many proofs in his letters of an ability for self-analysis, but it is of a detached and clinical sort, uncoloured by prejudice, touchiness or self-love. Nor was his self-knowledge distorted, as it was with Shelley, by an excessive preoccupation with the public or messianic rôle of the poet. No one was more purely or deeply dedicated to his art than Keats; yet he could write on occasion, 'I am sometimes so very sceptical as to think Poetry itself a mere Jack a lanthern to amuse whoever may chance to be struck with its brilliance';[6] or again, 'For although I take poetry (of the) Chief, there is something else wanting to one who passes his life among Books and thoughts on Books.'[7] The tone of these remarks is as significant as the overt burden. In the one the nicely sceptical, lightly ridiculing note gives the impression of being the utterance of a sane and realistic mind. In the other the deliberate and reflective air of the judgement endorses the suggestion that there must be more than poetry to make the full life. In both we see poetry and the vocation of poet accepted as serious and important, and yet placed in a larger hierarchy.

The general characteristics of Keats's self-awareness are both humorous sanity and humility, a combination which permitted him a sturdy independence of merely fashionable influences or ill-disposed critics. 'I refused to visit Shelley that I might have my own unfettered scope,'[8] he wrote on one occasion; and later in the year, 'My own domestic criticism has given me pain without comparison beyond what Blackwood or the [Edinburgh] Quarterly could possibly inflict, and also when I feel I am right, no external praises can give me such a glow as my own solitary reperception & ratification of what is fine.'[9] Its particular features are quickness in recognizing the mixtures of motives which impelled him and willingness not to rush to tidy them up into a neat and 'rational' pattern. He was confident enough to let his thoughts and motives lie in their puzzling ambiguity and patient enough not to thrust them into a false coherence. He could see the inadequacy of a Dilke 'who cannot feel he has a personal identity unless he has made up his Mind about every thing. . . . Dilke will never come at a truth as long as he lives; because he is always trying at it.'[10]

The habit of mind revealed in these remarks derives from a fundamental quality of Keats's genius, a scrupulous fidelity to the object of attention whether this be a landscape, or a constellation of feeling as in a poem, or the temperament displayed in a quarrel between Reynolds and Haydon. It is perhaps not without significance that what I have called the *object* of attention Keats should habitually refer to as the *subject*. Poetry itself, he generalized, 'should be great & unobtrusive, a thing which enters into one's soul, and does not startle it or amaze it with itself but with its subject'.[11] When he was conscious that he was deserting the subject, he rebuked himself in terms which show that keeping to it was for him a principle of his own intellectual life and a mark by which he judged the quality of other minds. 'I am continually running away from the subject – sure this cannot be exactly the case with a complex Mind – one that is imaginative and at the same time careful of its fruits – who would exist partly on sensation partly on thought.'[12]

The next six months, from January to June 1818, were a most significant period in Keats's intellectual formation. His conscious aim, he said, was 'to follow Solomon's directions of "get Wisdom – get understanding" '.[13] The complex mind he aimed at, the mind both imaginative and careful, existing both on sensation and thought, was being developed not in retirement but amid a social whirl, the professional business in preparing the *Endymion* manuscript, emending and correcting proofs, in study and continued attendance at Hazlitt's lectures, and disturbed by painful anxieties caused by Tom Keats's declining health. George, who was looking after Tom at Teignmouth, planned to convert the money left him by their grandmother, Mrs Jennings, to marry and emigrate to the United States. (Neither George nor Tom, as Gittings explains,[14] knew about another fund their grandfather had set up for them in Chancery, which for some unaccountable reason neither the family lawyer nor Abbey had advised them of.) George's plans were a further anxiety for Keats. Towards the end of February Keats found that he was expected to relieve George in looking after his brother Tom, and he left London in early March. He dashed down a hasty preface for *Endymion* which his publishers sensibly rejected on the grounds that its self-deprecating tone was likely to put off the reader and that several of the phrases would annoy the reviewers:

> I would fain escape the bickerings that all works not exactly in chime, bring upon their begetters, – but this is not fair to expect, there must be conversation of some sort and to object shows a man's consequence. In case of a London drizzle or a Scotch Mist, the following quotation from Marston may perhaps 'stead me as an umbrella for an hour or so: 'Let it be the Curtesy of my peruser rather to pity my self hindering labours than to malice me;'[15]

It was necessary for him to write and send a second, slimmer one, which he did by by 10 April. He was writing 'Isabella, or the Pot of Basil', a versification of one of Boccaccio's stories, and that too was finished by the end of April, at about the time *Endymion* was published.

It was during this stay that he was writing some of his most profound letters like the superb literary–psychological one to Reynolds on 3 May – to which I shall recur. He left Teignmouth with Tom early in May and was back in London on 11 May, having found Devonshire mixed in its pleasures: 'The Climate here weighs us [down] completely – Tom is quite low spirited – It is impossible to live in a country which is continually under hatches.'[16] On 29 May George married Georgiana Wylie, a girl John found himself much taken with. Keats was now thinking of his next major composition, *Hyperion*, which he first mentioned to Haydon at the end of January: 'In Endymion I think you may have many bits of the deep and sentimental cast – the nature of *Hyperion* will lead me to treat it in a more naked and grecian Manner – and the march of passion and endeavour will be undeviating.'[17]

Study and travel were prominent items in Keats's schedule of improvement: 'I purpose within a Month to put my knapsack at my back and make a pedestrian tour through the North of England, and part of Scotland – to make a sort of Prologue to the Life I intend to pursue – that is to write, to study and to see all Europe at the lowest expence.'[18] Tom's illness and the problems of seeing *Endymion* into print made him uncertain about this trip and he changed his mind more than once. But he was encouraged to go by the sensitive, self-sacrificing Tom, and having managed to extract five hundred pounds from Abbey, the last substantial amount he got from him, he left for the North in company with Brown, travelling to Liverpool with George and Georgiana who were to sail from there to Philadelphia. He saw George only once again and Georgiana never. George himself died a prosperous man, of tuberculosis, at the age of fifty-five (in Louisville, Kentucky).

Brown was a tough, energetic, loyal, amiable man, with a business background and artistic tastes. He was one of the most faithful if not most sensitive of Keats's friends. He and Keats made their difficult way to Ambleside to find that Wordsworth, who had earlier left London in a huff according to Keats,[19] was canvassing for the local Tory candidate, Parliament having been dissolved on 10 June[20] ('sad – sad – sad,' said Keats). Keats was entranced with the mountain scenery. 'I live in the eye; and my imagination, surpassed, is at rest.'[21] He made this comment after one of those marvellous descriptions of the place which filled his letters to Tom:

> First we stood a little below the head about half way down the first fall, buried deep in trees, and saw it streaming down two more descents to the depth of near fifty feet – then we went on a jut of rock nearly level with the second fall-head, where the first

> fall was above us, and the third below our feet still – at the same time we saw that the water was divided by a sort of cataract island on whose other side burst out a glorious stream – then the thunder and the freshness. At the same time the different falls have as different characters; the first darting down the slate-rock like an arrow; the second spreading out like a fan – the third dashed into a mist – and the one on the other side of the rock a sort of mixture of all these. We afterwards moved away a space, and saw nearly the whole more mild, streaming silverly through the trees.[22]

In Cumberland he admired the lively folk and their dances:

> We are this morning at Carlisle – After Skiddaw, we walked to Ireby the oldest market town in Cumberland – where we were greatly amused by a country dancing school, holden at the Inn, it was indeed 'no new cotillon fresh from France.' No they kickit & jumpit with mettle extraordinary, & whiskit, & flecket, & toe'd it, & go'd it, & twirld it, & wheel'd it, & stamp it, & sweated it, tattooing the floor like mad.[23]

In Dumfries Keats paid his respects at Burns's tomb, although the tomb itself was not much to his taste. They sailed from Port Patrick on the mailboat to Donaghadee, and Keats noted how much more cheerful were the chambermaids who were already ready to laugh, being 'out of the horrible dominion of the Scotch kirk'.[24] At the same time he was appalled by the misery, the dirt, and the barbarous conditions of the poor, common Irish, the horror of which he saw concentrated in one dreadful old woman. The sight of her turned his habitual appreciation of the grotesque into nightmare:

> On our return from Bellfast we met a Sadan – the Duchess of Dunghill – It is no laughing matter tho – Imagine the worst dog kennel you ever saw placed upon two poles from a mouldy fencing – In such a wretched thing sat a squalid old Woman squat like an ape half starved from a scarcity of Buiscuit in its passage from Madagascar to the cape, – with a pipe in her mouth and looking out with a round-eyed skinny lidded, inanity – with a sort of horizontal idiotic movement of her head – squab and lean she sat and puff'd out the smoke while two ragged tattered Girls carried her along – What a thing would be a history of her Life and sensations.[25]

Hard walking for nearly seven weeks, interspersed with stiff climbing, including Ben Nevis – for Keats shirked nothing – comfortless lodgings, coarse food – 'cursed oat cake' – left Keats exhausted and ill. A sore throat developed into tonsillitis and when he arrived in Inverness the local doctor firmly advised him to break off his trip. He returned to London by boat from Cromarty on 8 August. The ten days' journey to London Bridge gave him some chance to recover. Mrs Dilke reported, 'John Keats arrived here last night, as brown and as shabby as you can imagine; scarcely any shoes left, his jacket all torn at the back, a fur cap, a great plaid, and his knapsack.'[26]

The purposes of Keats's Scottish trip, he said, had been to 'give me more experience, rub off more Prejudice, use [me] to more hardship, identify finer scenes load me with grander Mountains and strengthen more my reach in Poetry'.[27] Certainly this hard, extremely physical excursion (the only book Keats took with him was Cary's translation of Dante, the only one Brown took was Milton) served several of these ends. The process of maturation, moral and poetic, was now to go on more profoundly and powerfully than ever. Experience was to be harsher and thought even more personal and creative. He found on his return that Tom was now extremely sick. Keats from now till Tom's death nursed him with a delicate and unremitting tenderness. His own health was still poor, and he continued to dose himself with large quantities of mercury, presumably on medical advice as a therapy against any development of his venereal disease. The lowering of his own health and the strain of nursing the uncomplaining Tom undoubtedly prepared his body to catch a tubercular infection. Again, shortly after his return, *Blackwood's Edinburgh Magazine* came out with the insulting attack on him,[28] a blend of abuse and self-indulgent bias, and the *Quarterly Review* made its own sour report. Here is a typical comment from *Blackwood's*:

> His friends, we understand, destined him to the career of medicine, and he was bound apprentice some years ago to a worthy apothecary in town. But all has been undone by a sudden attack of the malady to which we have alluded. Whether Mr. John has been sent home with a diuretic or composing draught to some patient far gone in the poetical mania, we have not heard. This much is certain, that he has caught the infection, and that thoroughly.[29]

And here one from the *Quarterly Review*:

> This author is a copyist of Mr. Hunt; but he is more unintelligible, almost as rugged, twice as diffuse, and ten times more tiresome and absurd than his prototype.[30]

Of the three matters agitating Keats at this period, health – Tom's and his own – was to provide a menacing context for all his creative work and personal life from now on. The response to his work by the reviewers, after the immediate upset, he took with admirable detachment. His inner sense, deriving from a profound artistic integrity, as to what was good, or weak, in his own work, meant far more to him than the reaction of the mediocre or the merely fashionable. The third of these matters was his relationships with women which proved to be awkward and troublesome for all his life.

> Is it not extraordinary? [he wrote to Bailey] When among Men I have no evil thoughts, no malice, no spleen – I feel free to speak or to be silent – I can listen and from every one I can learn – my hands are in my pockets I am free from all suspicion and comfortable. When I am among Women I have evil thoughts, malice spleen – I cannot speak or be silent – I am full of Suspicions and therefore listen to no thing – I am in a hurry to be gone – You must be charitable and put all this perversity to my being disappointed since Boyhood.[31]

Keats was deeply attached to his mother whom he guarded during his school days with ferocious intensity in her last illness. Her curious and hasty second marriage distressed him and her death that shattered the family circle scarred him permanently. He wanted to be close to his sister but this became more and more impossible because of the jealous guardianship of Abbey which, Bate[32] shrewdly guesses, was as much motivated by the desire to keep Keats in ignorance about the family inheritance as by moral doubts about the quality of Keats's friends. His very attachment to his brothers, the product of his early life, itself worked against easy, natural relations with women. 'I have two Brothers,' he wrote to Bailey, 'one is driven by the "burden of Society" to America the other, with an exquisite love of Life, is in a lingering state – My Love for my Brothers from the early loss of our parents and even for earlier Misfortunes has grown into a affection "passing the Love of Women" – I have been ill temper'd with them, I have vex'd them – but the thought of them has always stifled the impression that any woman might otherwise have made upon me.'[33] (Nor, I suppose, should we forget that Keats, though perfectly formed and strikingly handsome, was barely more than five feet tall, and by no means insensitive to his lack of height.)

One of the few women with whom Keats had an unclouded and simple relationship was George's wife Georgiana, 'a most disinterested girl', he said. Towards the end of October he met again Mrs Isabella Jones. He had some modestly romantic encounter, nothing more, with her about a year before when he met her at Hastings either in late May or early June. She was a handsome, independent and impressive woman. 'The Eve of St Agnes' was written on her suggestion, as was probably 'The Eve of St Mark'. According to Gittings,

> her rooms, which Keats visited frequently in the winter of 1818–19, are portrayed in the description of the room of the heroine, Bertha. There is also strong evidence that Isabella is the 'Isabel' of the lively lyric *Hush, hush*!, written at about this time, and, strongest of all, that the first version of Keats's sonnet *Bright Star* coincides with the reappearance in his life of this enigmatic and beautiful young woman.[34]

Keats himself writes to George and his wife about Mrs Jones and her rooms:

> Our Walk ended in 34 Gloucester Street Queen Square – not exactly so for we went up stairs into her sitting room – a very tasty sort of place with Books, Pictures a bronze statue of Buonaparte, Music, aeolian Harp; a Parrot a Linnet – A Case of choice Liquers &c &c &c. she behaved in the kindest manner – made me take home a Grouse for Tom's dinner – Asked for my address for the purpose of sending more game – As I had warmed with her before and kissed her – I though[t] it would be living backwards not to do so again – she had a better taste; she perceived how much a thing of course it was and shrunk from it – not in a prudish way but as in I say a good taste – She cont[r]ived to disappoint me in a way which made me feel more pleasure than a simple kiss could do – she said I should please her much more if I would only press her hand and go away.[35]

She insisted that her relationship with Keats be kept a secret from their friends, and Keats appears to have obeyed this injunction. Isabella Jones was connected with a prominent Irish Whig family and either the close friend or more probably, surely, the mistress of one of them, Donal O'Callaghan. In his *John Keats: The Living Year*, Gittings prints a letter from her to John Taylor in which she speaks of Severn's description of Keats's death. It is an impatient and vivacious document, touched with a near Augustan distaste for sentimentality when it refers to Severn's account of Keats's death:

> Of all the cants, in this canting world the cant of sentiment is the most disgusting and I never saw better specimens than these letters afford – they are extremely well got up and will impose upon the most literate – but do let me flatter myself that, *we* carry a test in the true feelings of *our* hearts, that exposes all such hollow pretensions – *His* own letter to Mr. B. [Brown] – with all its quaintness and harmless conceit is worth a waggon load of Mr. Egotist's productions.[36]

The second woman who affected Keats at this time was Jane Cox, a smoulderingly beautiful, intelligent girl. 'She is not a Cleopatra;' Keats wrote, 'but she is at least a Charmian. She has a rich eastern look; she has fine eyes and fine manners. When she comes into a room she makes an impression the same as the Beauty of a Leopardess.'[37] He wasn't in love with her, he told George, but 'she kept me awake one Night as a tune of Mozart's might do'.[38] If he wasn't in love with her, he was certainly in a state to be in love. In fact he was in love very soon after meeting Fanny Brawne, which he did in late November of this year. Tom was sinking, and Keats was composing *Hyperion*. The pull of death against the attraction of life was a deep, constitutive tension in Keats's experience and his art. *Hyperion*, while it did not itself attain it, except perhaps in patches, helped towards the living equilibrium of the two he achieved finally in the great Odes. He did not succeed in arriving at anything as satisfying in his personal life. Nor had Fanny the resources either of character or feeling to help him to do so: something for which as an inexperienced girl of eighteen she can hardly be blamed. The Brawnes – or at least the husband Samuel, the mother had grander connections – came from a lower-middle-class background not unlike Keats's own. Samuel Brawne had even kept an inn at one time. When he died – again it was from tuberculosis – he left a widow and three children, Fanny who was now eighteen, Samuel fourteen, Margaret nine, and very little else. Mrs Brawne's income came from a deceased brother. Brown had let Mrs Brawne his Wentworth Place house when he went with Keats to Scotland. On his return the Brawnes took lodgings nearby at Downshire Hill, and when in the spring of 1819 the Dilkes moved to Westminster, the Brawnes rented Dilke's house. When Tom – poor Tom – died on 1 December 1819 Keats moved next door to them as a paying guest with Brown. Nothing would be more natural than that the acquaintance should rapidly ripen into love. Fanny, although she had a touch of the positive and independent quality of Isabella Jones and Jane Cox, was quite unlike them. Immature where they were poised, pretty where they were beautiful, she had few intellectual tastes and little interest in poetry. She was by no means unintelligent and developed in her maturity, when she lived in Europe with her husband Louis Lindo, a gift for languages and a shrewd financial sense. At this time she preferred chat and clothes to poetry and philosophy.

Fanny's first impressions of John are cooler but less observant than his. She remembered years later that 'his conversation was in the highest degree interesting, and his spirits good, excepting at moments when anxiety regarding his brother's health dejected them'.[39] They do, however, convey a sense of the reserved courage with which Keats bore himself in his anguish at Tom's plight. Keats's own reaction is sharper, and it includes the note of irritated fascination their relationship was never really to be free of:

> Mrs Brawne who took Brown's house for the Summer, still resides in Hampstead – she is a very nice woman – and her daughter senior is I think beautiful and elegant, graceful, silly, fashionable and strange – we have a little tiff now and then – and she behaves a little better, or I must have sheered off.[40]

Two days later he writes about her again:

> Shall I give you Miss Brawn? She is about my height – with a fine style of countenance of the lengthen'd sort – she wants sentiment in every feature – she manages to make her hair look well – her nostrils are fine – through a little painful – her mouth is bad and good – her Profil is better than her full-face which indeed is not full but pale and thin without showing any bone – Her shape is very graceful and so are her movements – her Arms are good, her hands badish – her feet tolerable – she is not seventeen [actually she was eighteen and three months] – but

> she is ignorant – monstrous in her behaviour flying out in all directions, calling people such names – that I was forced lately to make use of the term *Minx* – this I think no[t] from any innate vice but from a penchant she has for acting stylishly.[41]

The next three months of Keats's life were at once a jumble of distractions and a period of extraordinary interior transformation. The shattering blow of Tom's death, no easier for being expected, was followed by the harassing business of settling Tom's estate.

> The last days of poor Tom were of the most distressing nature; but his last moments were not so painful and his very last was without a pang – I will not enter into any parsonic comments on death – yet the common observations of the commonest people on death are as true as their proverbs. I have scarce a doubt of immortality of some nature of other – neither had Tom.[42]

Keats's throat trouble, which seems to have been becoming chronic, still bothered him. *Hyperion* was hanging fire, and his second volume had evoked as poor a response from the reading public as his first. It even flashed through his mind to take up medicine again. His friends had entertained him almost frantically after Tom's death but he resolved to give up 'traipsing' and concentrate on his own work. Haydon, as usual hard up, was pressing him for money. The suspicious and curmudgeonly Abbey opposed Keats's desire to be closer to his sister Fanny. He visited Covent Garden with Rice and Reynolds, and the British Museum with Severn. He had reached an understanding with Fanny Brawne on Christmas Day and he followed this with a visit to Chichester to Dilke's parents where he stayed with Brown and wrote 'The Eve of St Agnes'.

In February he began 'The Eve of St Mark' but never finished it. He continued with his reading which now included Voltaire and American history. Anxious for exercise he played cricket on 18 March, was hit by a ball and got his second black eye since leaving school, and was given a little opium to relieve it. During March and the first fortnight of April he complained constantly of his 'indolence' as he called it. 'I have written nothing, and almost read nothing – but I must turn over a new leaf,'[43] he wrote to his sister Fanny on 12 April. The day before, he had had an accidental meeting with Coleridge, a strange encounter of which we have a comic report from Keats and a gloomy comment from Coleridge. First of all, Keats:

> I walked with him at his alderman-after dinner pace for near two miles I suppose. In those two Miles he broached a thousand things – let me see if I can give you a list – Nightingales, Poetry – on Poetical sensation – Metaphysics – Different genera and species of Dreams – Nightmare – a dream accompanied by a sense of touch – single and double touch – A dream related – First and second consciousness – the difference explained between will and Volition – so many metaphysicians from a want of smoking the second consciousness – Monsters – the Kraken – Mermaids – southey believes in them – southeys belief too much diluted – A ghost story – Good morning – I heard this voice as he came towards me – I heard it as he moved away – I had heard it all the interval – if it may be called so. He was civil enough to ask me to call on him at Highgate.[44]

And from Coleridge:

> A loose, slack, not well-dressed youth met Mr.— and myself in a lane near Highgate. — knew him, and spoke. It was Keats. He was introduced to me, and stayed a minute or so. After he had left us a little way, he came back and said, 'Let me carry away the memory, Coleridge, of having pressed your hand!' – 'There is death in that hand,' I said to —, when Keats was gone; yet this was, I believe, before the consumption showed itself distinctly.[45]

This sad, busy, frustrating part of his life ended suddenly. He gave up *Hyperion* and in a single day, 21 April, he wrote 'La Belle Dame sans Merci'. This exquisitely poised and delicately individual poem, the begetter and the unattainable ideal of so much pre-Raphaelite art, is a marvellous illustration of the truly creative mind. It is thronged with literary echoes, resonances, and sources, and in one sense it could hardly be less original if it had set out to collect and incorporate 'influences'. In the immediate background are Wordsworth, Coleridge and Cary's translation of Dante, then Scott and Percy's *Reliques of Ancient Poetry*, and further back William Brown, Robert Burton, Spenser and the medieval French poet Alain Chartier. And yet it transcends all that it came from and is uniquely Keats's own, both in substance and voice. The rhythm with its minimum of conditions is mobile and unclogged, and the usual simple ballad line, the alternation of four and three beats, disposed into two phrasal units, is given Keats's own modification into a fourth line of a double and strongly stressed beat. It is a rhythm which is spare enough in action and never far enough from the movement of speech, into which it can fall with perfect naturalness. As to what the poem means, it seems to me wholly wrong to attempt, as some do, to offer a prose paraphrase of some extractable significance. Its meaning cannot be equated with the sterility of lust, with a siren principle of female destructiveness, or even taken to be an analogue of Keats's relationship with Fanny Brawne. No doubt each of these notions is either faintly or more positively present here or there in the poem. But while its meaning cannot, as I shall argue with respect to 'To Autumn' later, be wholly bleached of thought, of theory, it cannot be phrased in terms of thought or theory in any way consonant with its complexity. Its meaning is really an attitude, a profound intuition about life, which shapes and turns and colours the images, the rhythm and the tone. At the heart of that attitude is a sense of the one unavoidable condition of existence, the inescapable, terrifying and hopeless grimness of reality. The pressure and the force of this conviction are all the more positive in a context of wonder and faery where it might have been thought not possible to admit it at all.

> Oh what can ail thee, knight-at-arms,
>   Alone and palely loitering?
> The sedge has withered from the lake,
>   And no birds sing.
>
> Oh what can ail thee, knight-at-arms,
>   So haggard and so woe-begone?
> The squirrel's granary is full,
>   And the harvest's done. . . .
>
> I met a lady in the meads,
>   Full beautiful – a faery's child,
> Her hair was long, her foot was light,
>   And her eyes were wild. . . .
>
> I saw pale kings and princes too,
>   Pale warriors, death-pale were they all;
> They cried – 'La Belle Dame sans Merci
>   Thee hath in thrall!'

I saw their starved lips in the gloam,
With horrid warning gapèd wide
And I awoke and found me here,
On the cold hill's side.

And this is why I sojourn here
Alone and palely loitering,
Though the sedge is withered from the lake,
And no birds sing.

Notes

1 *Champion*, 21 December 1817.
2 *Letters*, I, pp. 386–7.
3 ibid., I, pp. 193–4.
4 ibid., p. 232.
5 ibid., p. 374.
6 ibid., p. 242.
7 ibid., p. 274.
8 ibid., p. 170.
9 ibid., p. 374.
10 ibid., II, p. 213.
11 ibid., I, p. 224.
12 ibid., pp. 185–6.
13 ibid., p. 271.
14 Cf. Gittings, *John Keats*, p. 196.
15 Cf. John Barnard, *John Keats, The Complete Poems* (Harmondsworth: Penguin, 2nd edn, 1976), p. 507.
16 *Letters*, I, p. 269.
17 ibid., p. 207
18 ibid., p. 264.
19 ibid., p. 265.
20 Cf. Eli Halévy, *A History of the English People in the Nineteenth Century*, vol. II (London: 1926), 2nd, rev. edn (London: Benn, 1949), p. 35.
21 *Letters*, I, p. 301.
22 ibid., pp. 300–1.
23 ibid., p. 307.
24 ibid., p. 319.
25 ibid., pp. 321–2.
26 ibid., p. 364 n.
27 ibid., p. 342.
28 A further attack followed in the same month in the *British Critic*.
29 *Blackwood's Edinburgh Magazine*, August 1818 (published 2 September).
30 *Quarterly Review*, April 1818 (published 27 September).
31 *Letters*, I, p. 341.
32 Cf. Bate, *John Keats*, p. 364.
33 *Letters*, I, p. 293.
34 Robert Gittings, *The Mask of Keats* (London: Heinemann, 1956), p. 45.
35 *Letters*, I, pp. 402–3.
36 Robert Gittings, *John Keats: The Living Year* (London: Heinemann, 1954), p. 232.
37 *Letters*, I, p. 395.
38 ibid., p. 395.
39 Gittings, *John Keats*, p. 263.

40 *Letters*, II, p. 8.
41 ibid., p. 13.
42 ibid., p. 4.
43 ibid., p. 51.
44 Bate, op. cit., p. 467.
45 *Table Talk*, 14 August 1832 (London: Walter Scott, 1894).

5
The education of sensibility

I

Some twenty years ago I wrote an essay on the development of Keats's sensibility.[1] I should like at this point, and again basing myself on Keats's letters, to summarize, correct, and amplify the argument advanced there. Between *Endymion* and the great Odes (April–May 1819) Keats was, it is clear, astonishingly transformed, advancing from the status of a gifted and charming minor talent to that of a major writer. As I see it, that development is in essence a brilliant, profound and exemplary exercise in self-education. I want, largely in Keats's own words, to trace the course of this development.

To begin with, there is the natural endowment of the poet, those elements and capacities of his nature which correspond to, and are a development of, the ordinary man's sense-apparatus and powers of perception and feeling, 'the knowledge of contrast, feeling for light and shade, all that information (primitive sense) necessary for a poem'.[2] The play of this primitive sense, however graceful, is limited in its ability to grapple with the complexities of reality and in its appeal to the responsible mind. The free flow of feeling has to be directed, tested and accounted for, or it becomes simply playful, charming and entertaining. It may be free but it is not disciplined; it may be attractive but it is not grown-up. No one in his personal life, no young poet in the practice of his art, becomes adult by the simple process of growth. At a certain point the man or the poet has to make a radical choice. It may be of the instantaneous Pauline kind or the slower distillation of a decision gradually, and almost insensibly, arrived at. To us Keats's decision seems like the first, a sudden and absolute vision, though to him who was so much less impressed than we by the unparalleled pace of his development, it looked like the second, a slow and painful process.

Keats saw the choice under a variety of forms. 'I think a little change has taken place in my intellect lately – I cannot bear to be uninterested or unemployed, I who for so long a time, have been addicted to passiveness.'[3] Or again: 'I hope I am a little more of a Philosopher than I was, consequently a little less of a versifying Pet-lamb.'[4] Or in another place: 'Some think I have lost that poetic ardour and fire 't is said I once had – the fact is perhaps I have: but instead of that I hope I shall substitute a more thoughtful and quiet power.'[5] Perhaps these words put the choice most nakedly: 'I must choose between despair and Energy – I choose the latter.'[6]

This is one of those decisions which is made even if one wants to abstain from making it. Not to make it is to opt for the other side. By this decision the artist decides for disinterestedness, devotion, seriousness, application, and against volatility, impulse and indiscipline. As Keats saw it, there are two modes of personal development for the artist, one moral, one intellectual. Sensibility itself, his letters constantly imply, is matured by becoming more tellingly infused by intellect and less precariously the instrument of morality.

In Keats's judgement these two, intellectual development and moral progress, are hardly to be distinguished one from the other. Morality became intellectually enlightened, intelligence strengthened by morality. Keats more than once made an explicit connection between them. He wrote, for example, 'I find that I can have no enjoyment in the World but continual drinking of Knowledge – I find there is no worthy pursuit but the idea of doing some good for the world.'[7] Upon this development, upon the increasingly intimate connection of knowledge and sensibility, depended the development of the poet himself. Sensibility, the intellect, the moral sense, develop as a single existence, flow in and out of one another till they are indistinguishable. Or in Keats's idiom: 'Then I should be most enviable – with the yearning Passion I have for the beautiful, connected and made one with the ambition of my intellect.'[8]

The mind which can only find enjoyment in drinking in knowledge and doing good in the world, which connects a passion for the beautiful with the ambition of the intellect, is distinguished by a certain bearing, a style which Whitehead defined as 'the ultimate morality of mind'. Keats does not specify the virtues of this style in a given place but they are distributed throughout his letters and they do combine in a coherent judgement. The first is the virtue of disinterestedness, the acceptance of a discipline or system which can never be compromised or sacrificed to the interest of something else. This is the primary virtue, the moral correlative of reason itself. As Keats said: 'for that sort of probity & disinterestedness which such men as Bailey possess, does hold & grasp the tip top of any spiritual honours, that can be paid to any thing in this world.'[9] Keats was also aware of the danger implicit in the hard and persevering labour of preserving integrity, namely that it itself should become an abstract godhead. Keats understood the danger of sacrificing one's humanity, and he expresses this with a characteristic combination of common sense, sincerity and steadiness of purpose. 'All I hope,' he says, 'is that I may not lose all interest in human affairs – that the solitary indifference I feel for applause even from the finest Spirits, will not blunt any acuteness of vision I may have.'[10]

On the one hand, then, there is the great intellectual virtue of probity and disinterestedness; on the other, its companion and discipline. This is a ripeness of tolerance, generosity, disillusion and a tonic sense of actuality. Here he brings the two themes together in a perfect balance:

> Men should bear with each other – there lives not the Man who may not be cut up, aye hashed to pieces on his weakest side. The best of Men have but a portion of good in them – a kind of spiritual yeast in their frames which creates the ferment of existence – by which a Man is propell'd to act and strive and buffet with Circumstance.[11]

And again we hear that experienced (though it was experience gained without the length of years) dismissal of the inflated pretensions of mankind.

> Very few men have ever arrived at a complete disinterestedness of Mind: very few have been influenced by a pure desire of the benefit of others – in the great part of the Benefactors [of] & to Humanity some meretricious motive has sullied their greatness – some melodramatic scenery has fascinated them.[12]

Nor did Keats's clear discernment of the mixture, the impurity of human motives, ever become an easy cynicism. He goes on: 'As Wordsworth says, "we have all one human heart" – there is an ellectric fire in human nature tending to purify – so that among these human creature[s] there is continually some birth of new heroism.'[13]

Keats's realistic diagnosis of human fact, his generous estimation of human possibility, gave him the soundest understanding of the substance of intellectual advance. But he had an equally shrewd insight into the tactics, roots and conditions of mental progress. By the following words he did not mean to plead for universal scepticism but rather for range, catholicity, deliberation and suspended judgement. Waiting upon the event had for Keats creative possibilities:

> The only means of strengthening one's intellect is to make up one's mind about nothing – to let the mind be a thoroughfare for all thoughts. Not a select party. . . . All the stubborn arguers you meet with are of the same brood – They never begin upon a subject they have not preresolved on.[14]

'An extensive knowledge is needful to thinking people', but there is no merit in it as such. It is an instrumental good; it is to be valued in Keats's view because 'it takes away the heat and fever; and helps, by widening speculation, to ease the Burden of the Mystery'.[15] On the other hand, an extensive knowledge, when it is enlightened and articulated, is a demonstration in one mind, or better, a minute exemplification of the unity of all knowledge. To be aware of this truth in an intimate and personal way ('for axioms in philosophy are not axioms until they are proved upon our pulses')[16] is both a stage in and sign of intellectual maturity. 'When the mind is in its infancy a Bias is in reality a Bias,' Keats says, 'but when we have acquired more strength, a Bias becomes no Bias. Every department of knowledge we see excellent and calculated towards a great whole.'[17]

The knowledge which exists in a given mind is, in an educated one, organized to some degree. That organization as Keats saw it invariably had one or two leading themes or interests: 'the two uppermost thoughts in a Man's mind are the two poles of his World he revolves on them and everything is southward or northward to him through their means – We take but three steps from feathers to iron.'[18] The intelligent acceptance of this limitation together with the sense of modesty and realism which it argues is a check to fanaticism: 'the points of leaves and twigs on which the Spider begins her work are few and she fills the Air with a beautiful circuiting. Man should be content with as few points to tip with the fine Webb of his Soul.'[19] Nor is this fact about the human mind anything which should lead to division either of man from man or of the specialist from the general body of the educated:

> But the Minds of Mortals are so different and bent on such diverse Journeys that it may at first appear impossible for any common taste and fellowship to exist between two or three under these suppositions – It is however quite the contrary – Minds would leave each other in contrary directions, traverse each other in Numberless points, and all [at] last greet each other at the Journeys end – An old Man and a child would talk together and the old Man be led on his Path, and the child left thinking – Man should not dispute or assert but whisper results to his neighbour, and thus by every germ of Spirit sucking the Sap from mould ethereal every human might become great, and Humanity instead of being a wide heath or Furse and Briars with here and there a remote Oak or Pine, would become a grand democracy of Forest Trees.[20]

Moreover, 'every point of thought', Keats insisted, 'is the centre of an intellectual world',[21] and 'When Man has arrived at a certain ripeness in intellect any one grand and spiritual passage serves him as a starting post towards all "the two-and thirty Pallaces" '.[22]

When he analysed his own arrival at a certain intellectual ripeness, Keats was apt to stress two contrary influences. In the first place he is very firm about the necessity for effort, will and energy. At one point he maintains that 'every mental pursuit takes its reality and worth from the ardour of the pursuer'. If he is so convinced about this it is in part to be attributed to a reaction from what he felt to be an undue bias in his own nature, namely an excessive susceptibility to the attraction of luxurious indolence. But Keats, as we have noted more than once, had that resilient and embracing quality of mind, which can see and use the other side of a question effectively. He therefore insisted, as we have noted before, on the importance in intellectual development of not forcing the issue, of patiently waiting upon the event. 'Nothing,' he wrote, 'is finer for the purpose of great productions, than a very gradual ripening of the intellectual powers.'[23] Again we observe that what to us seems to be his incredible rapidity of growth, appears to him as a grudgingly and painfully gained progress. So that to advance intellectually the artist required ardour and energy and also the quality he termed Negative Capability, which is partly defined as the 'absence of any irritable reaching after fact and reason', the capacity to be still and receptive without any 'buzzing here and there for a knowledge of what is to be arrived at'. The ability to attend calmly on the gradual ripening of the powers of the mind is the intellectual equivalent of an attribute we find repeatedly referred to in Keats's letters as proper to a mature mind. That is the virtue of a rational humility. I say 'rational' because there is nothing servile or unmanly in Keats's idea of humility. 'I have not,' he writes, 'the slightest feel of humility towards the Public – or to anything in existence, – but the eternal Being, the Principle of Beauty – and the Memory of great Men.'[24] Humility, as Keats understood it, was positive and selective, neither a mere absence of pride nor a generalized feeling of inferiority. But if he stood in a position of dignified independence towards his audience, his attitude to it was also free from any infection of arrogance. 'I have not the least contempt for my species; and though it may sound paradoxical: my greatest elevation of soul leave[s] me every time more humbled.'[25] To be humble towards those with a more inclusive view of life and finer vision of perfection, Keats thought, was to preserve the health of one's soul with the salt of sanity. Without it, a man was guilty of a mortal sin. 'There is no greater Sin after the 7 deadly than to flatter one-self into an idea of being a great Poet – or one of those beings who are privileged to wear out their Lives in the pursuit of Honor.'[26] And since humility is a wide-eyed view of reality, to be without it is also to fall into the illusory and the unreal. 'Every man has his speculations, but every man does not brood and peacock over them till he makes a false coinage and deceives himself.'[27]

Humility, or an unclouded sense of reality, was an attribute of the mature mind, and part of the criterion by which Keats tended to separate, in his own judgements of others, mind from mind. Other notes in this distinction he gives in another letter, where he distinguishes the immature from the serious, the superficial from the deeply disciplined mind:

> . . . there are two distinct tempers of mind in which we judge of things – the worldly, theatrical and pantomimical; and the unearthly, spiritual and etherial – in the former Buonapart, Lord Byron and this Charmian hold the first place in our Minds; in the latter John Howard, Bishop Hooker rocking his child's cradle and you my dear Sister, are the conquering feelings.[28]

A further attribute of intellectual fulfilment he gave in a negative way. Of his contemporary Dilke he said once that he was 'a Godwin-perfectibility man',[29] that is, possessed of an unreal and euphoric sense of the millennium to be achieved by purely political or scientific action. Keats himself was not, nor anyone he approved of, 'a Godwin-perfectibility man'. 'But in truth,' he said, 'I do not at all believe in this sort of perfectibility – the nature of the world will not admit of it – the inhabitants of the world will correspond to itself.'[30]

Keats certainly held to a qualified Whig view of progress. There had been, he believed, between Milton and Wordsworth 'a grand march of intellect'. But he had no unqualified optimism about human progress. He was distinctly critical of the religious mind but he had this in common with it, a disbelief that the most liberal intentions and the best of good will could ever usher in an earthly paradise. Human nature had a certain constancy and permanence and human experience was always liable to be strained by tension and conflict. His conception of human nature and his reading of human life were, indeed, integral with those that we find in the greatest literature. He held the tragic view of human life. It modified his attitude to practical affairs and it was the principle under which he organized his picture of the human situation.

> I will put down a simile of human life as far as I now perceive it; that is, to the point to which I say we both have arrived at – Well – I compare human life to a large Mansion of Many Apartments, two of which I can only describe, the doors of the rest being as yet shut upon me – The first we step into we call the infant or thoughtless Chamber, in which we remain as long as we do not think – We remain there a long while, and notwithstanding the doors of the second Chamber remain wide open, showing a bright appearance, we care not to hasten to it; but are at length imperceptibly impelled by the awakening of the thinking principle – within us – we no sooner get into the second Chamber, which I shall call the Chamber of Maiden-Thought, than we become intoxicated with the light and the atmosphere, we see nothing but pleasant wonders, and think of delaying there for ever in delight: However among the effect this breathing is father of is that tremendous one of sharpening one's vision into the heart and nature of Man – of convincing one's nerves that the

> World is full of Misery and Heartbreak, Pain, Sickness and oppression – whereby This Chamber of Maiden-Thought becomes gradually darken'd and at the same time on all sides of it many doors are set open – but all dark – all leading to dark passages – We see not the ballance of good and evil. We are in a mist – *We* are now in that state – We feel the 'burden of the Mystery'.[31]

In this astonishing statement Keats sees the individual's life in a way reminiscent both of the Bible and Shakespeare – if I may be so bold as to put it like this – as a mixed metaphor. It is both a many-roomed mansion and a journey: in fact, a house to be explored. The first room, or the first phase, is occupied by the fluent and graceful play of the unthinking mind. The second, in which we become increasingly and intensely aware of the glittering marvels of existence – the second chamber – we come to after the awakening within us of the thinking principle – that is, after the realization that we have to make a fundamental decision between youthful play and adult work. We see how in the first chamber, or the first phase, the individual soul registers, more or less passively, the bright appearances of existence; in the second, the individual, or his will, is the active and initiating influence. The discipline of refining one's sensual vision follows upon the awakening of the thinking principle, and it entails developing the virtues of disinterestedness, humility and a sense of reality. Essential to this undertaking is the capacity to discern the tragic nature of human life, of 'convincing one's nerves that the World is full of Misery and Heartbreak, Pain, Sickness and oppression'. Man is to be seen as at least potentially responsible and moral and therefore tragic and not wholly passive, conformist and perfectible. It is thus that we establish a sense of identity; it is thus that a person becomes 'personally itself'. For Keats the world was a place in which we alter nature, constructing from our experience a personal identity, a school in which we make an intelligence into a soul. Human life was 'a vale of soul making'.

II

When I reflect on the argument advanced so far, I recognize that it has addressed itself more to the intellectual and moral context of the development of Keats's sensibility and much less to the immediate development of that sensibility. This procedure derives no doubt from the conviction which has been expressed by Santayana that mere sensation or mere emotion is an indignity to a mature human being. Sensibility has its moral and intellectual grounds, connections and warrants. If it did not it would simply be a talent for dreaming, and 'Art, so long as it needs to be a dream,' Santayana says, 'will never cease to prove a disappointment. Its facile cruelty, its narcotic abstraction, can never sweeten the evils we return to at home; it can liberate half the mind only by leaving the other half in abeyance.'[32] This quotation is given not simply to explain the assumptions from which my own argument derives, but also, of course, because it states exactly part of the weakness of Keats's own sensibility, and part of what it needed most to overcome in its growth towards maturity. Moreover, it is not sufficient to suggest, as I seem to have been doing, that moral and intellectual growth on their own will necessarily foster sensibility. They are essential but not sufficient. Sensibility has its own intrinsic vitality. 'The Genius of Poetry must work out its own salvation in a man: It cannot be matured by law & precept, but by sensation & watchfulness in itself.'[33]

In the same letter Keats tells us what he saw, given the original poetic faculty, i.e. the primitive sense 'necessary for a poem', as the first steps towards its development, namely independence and courage. The weakness of *Endymion* is to be attributed in Keats's eyes precisely to his being unwilling to accept any help and to insisting on writing it independently:

> Had I been nervous about its being a perfect piece, & with that view asked advice, & trembled over every page, it would not have been written; for it is not in my nature to fumble – I will write independently. . . . In Endymion, I leaped headlong into the Sea, and thereby have become better acquainted with the Soundings, the quicksands, & the rocks, than if I had [stayed] upon the green shore, and piped a silly pipe, and took tea & comfortable advice. – I was never afraid of failure.[34]

Keats always exhibited exemplary courage, whether in facing personal disaster or sustaining disappointment and pain, and his independence is shown in his fierce rejection of patronage and in his faith in his own talent. Although 'as we grow older', he observed, 'each follows with more precision the bent of his own mind',[35] his own career reflected the succession found in many creative artists, a sequence made up of three phases, first – and in spite of his declared independence of character – that in which he was the imitator, second that in which he was the learner, and third that in which he was the practitioner. In Keats's case these phases or stresses, while they did not neatly follow one another, are severally associated with a dominant author, the imitator with Spenser, the learner with Milton and the practitioner with Shakespeare.

Spenser was for Keats what Eliot was for many young poets in England between the wars, both a provocation to write and an establisher of the assumptions and idiom of poetry. Cowden Clarke reminds us how he and Keats used to read *The Faerie Queene* and the *Epithalamion* after he had left school, when he was in his apprenticeship with Thomas Hammond. Keats, indeed, felt in Spenser a vigour which it is hard for us to appreciate now. He would go through Spenser, Cowden Clarke remembered, 'as a young horse would through a spring meadow – ramping! . . . He hoisted himself up, and looked burly and dominant, as he said, "what an image that is – '*sea-shouldering whales*!' " '.[36] It was a vignette of Spenser that appeared on the title page of his first book. His first poem was an 'Imitation of Spenser'. 'Mrs Tighe and Beattie', the eighteenth-century Spenserians, 'once delighted me', he confessed. It was Spenser he quoted before he began that distinctly Spenserian poem *Endymion*. Keats loved in Spenser the combination of freshness, fullness and musicality, the

> Spenserian vowels that elope with ease,
> And float along like birds o'er summer seas.

In Keats's nature there was developed to the point of extremity what exists in us all to some degree – a capacity to be aware of the existence of things, the force with which objects occupy their particular pool of vacancy. In Keats this instinct was a passion. He felt the weight and pressure of things, the intensities of existence, as though things did not simply stand on their own but leaned on him. For him, therefore, the senses serving immediacy, the sense of taste, the sense of touch, had a peculiar importance. He could be tinglingly alive to sense-experience and simultaneously drown in it. It was both life and death to him. In Spenser he discerned, in a way that is puzzling to us now, the instinct for embodied existence given the form of art. But Keats was not simply the man who longed for a life of sensation rather than thought, or one who hungered after sensation rather than truth. He had an original and gifted mind with a strong English pragmatic bent which meant he was a thinker rather than an intellectual. It was not surprising, therefore, that he should want his art as it developed to correspond both with the powerfully sensory and the strenuously thinking sides of his nature. It was Milton, and to a lesser degree Wordsworth, who influenced him in fostering this development.

It was Milton, rather than Wordsworth, that Keats chose as the model from whom he hoped to learn how to enlarge his poetic universe with a philosophical dimension, and from whom he hoped to learn to charge his more indolent style with a new kind of force. John Jones says, '. . . he has to choose between condemning his own poetry to the function of Flora-and-Pan escapism and forming the abstract–ambitious resolve to answer that same question satisfactorily. In *Hyperion* he very deliberately accepts the second alternative . . .'.[37] And 'The subsequent study of Milton gave his mind a mighty addition of energy & manly vigour, which stand out so nobly in Hyperion', as Bailey reported. The seed of *Hyperion* was embedded in *Endymion*, its sources much the same as that poem's, and its theme was the inevitable displacement of the superannuated. Although Keats was no Godwin-perfectibility man, he had a sturdily English and protestant belief in 'the general and gregarious advance of intellect', which for example could account in his view for Wordsworth's superiority over Milton in sensitivity of insight into the nature of man. It was not surprising, therefore, that evolution should appeal as a theme to him, or that he should light upon the machinery of the old gods' displacement by the new as an appropriate vehicle, or that given all this he should choose to cultivate austere, Miltonic or Dantesque grandeur.

It is easy to see why Milton should have appealed as a model to a poet of Keats's character, and one engaged like Keats in an effort, intense and sustained, 'to refine his sensual vision'. (Not that Milton appeared as an artist actually undergoing this process of self-redemption, but rather that he showed what might be hoped for at the end of it.) There was a strong Miltonic current running in the eighteenth century, especially among those minor writers who were later to be thought of as writers of 'true poetry', the predecessors of Romanticism. Then, with the rejection of Augustanism, Milton came to stand for all that was lofty, epic and severe in the English tradition. He was the solitary giant, looming and self-sufficient, and the distracted second-generation

Romantics were profoundly impressed by his heroic individuality, his calm assumption of the poet's public robes, and the untroubled confidence with which he undertook his enormous theme. Above all he represented a poet in his rôle as moral teacher and spiritual healer.

Hyperion, written between September and December 1818, mostly while Keats was nursing the dying Tom, exhibits and ministers to his extraordinary virtuosity. In rhythm, idiom, in pacing, in language poetically removed as far as possible from the staple of ordinary speech, it is an immensely more Miltonic production than anything in the eighteenth century. That it should be a narrative in spite of his own predilection for and ambition in respect of the drama, was something else he learnt both from Milton and from Wordsworth himself, who believed that in the circumstances of the nineteenth century the true voice of the poet was the narrative not the dramatic. What Keats learnt actively and positively from Milton during *Hyperion* was balanced by a gain in negative and critical learning. It is true that the abstract and impersonal in *Hyperion* served to soften the misery of attending to his dying brother, but he was increasingly disturbed by a purpose, so loftily impersonal as to be at odds with the bias of his own nature, about a fiction which had neither the complexity nor the possibilities of growth in it to sustain the narrative and about the means, the remote Miltonic idiom, in which it was to be realized. If he increased in ease and authority, in virtuosity and command, as he did, and thereby enabled himself to open a year of unprecedented creativity, during which he would finally become the Shakespearean practitioner, he was also uneasy about Miltonic verse, about its non-English character, about its foreign inversions and artful manner. If *Paradise Lost* was a corruption of our language, 'a beautiful and grand curiosity', then how much more must this be true of an imitation, however fine, and however inward. *Hyperion* itself was given up in April or May, and work on *The Fall of Hyperion* which he began later in the summer ceased on 21 September. 'Life to him would be death to me.' A discrepancy lies at the heart of *Hyperion*. It was intended to be an extension of Keats's poetic experience, an effort in a new direction, and also a stage in his spiritual progress, an exercise in moral discipline; in fact, it turned out to be a contraction of the one and a retrogressive step in the case of the other. What was meant to be as strict and ascetic as Milton proved to be as ornamental as Spenser, as relaxed as Tennyson. What was designed to be a central commentary on human life disclosed itself as merely marginal and elegiac, not a vehicle for wisdom but a symptom of uncertainty.

According to Leavis the revision was an attempt to graft the poem on to Keats's own maturer personality, but it was a failure, 'The new life is confined to the three hundred added lines of induction, which, however, suffice for a conclusive effect.'[38] Here is an example of the new life to which Leavis refers:

> Fanatics have their dreams, wherewith they weave
> A paradise for a sect; The savage too
> From forth the loftiest fashion of his sleep
> Guesses at heaven; pity these have not
> Traced upon vellum or wild Indian leaf
> The shadows of melodious utterance,
> But bare of laurel they live, dream and die.

The tone of this passage has the unmistakable note of authority, the unstrained confidence belonging to a mind fully in possession of an idea, and aware with precision of its every implication. The opening announcement 'Fanatics have their dreams', is made with axiomatic certainty, and the body of the piece follows with the firmness of a logical conclusion. There is a significant structural alteration within the first four lines. The phrase 'wherewith they weave / A paradise for a sect' follows unbrokenly on the first completed general statement; the corresponding phrase 'From forth the loftiest fashion of his sleep' is interpolated into the second general statement, 'The savage too / Guesses at heaven'. The lines begin with an unqualified statement, are then enriched by the detail of two supporting but contrasting phrases – there is an element of deliberate design in 'wherewith they weave' opposed to the uncalculated process of 'From forth the loftiest fashion of his sleep' – and comes to an end again on an unconditioned fact. The effect of certitude anchored in particulars is corroborated by the varying inflections of the rhythm. The pulse at first is strong and regular, quickens at 'wherewith they weave', slows at 'the savage too', accelerates for 'From forth the loftiest fashion of his sleep', and diminishes its pace to a collected conclusion with 'Guesses at heaven'. At the same time the sudden inversion of the beat at 'guesses' pulls the reader up, and subtly recalls the effort of the savage's guessing. The dry regret compressed into one word, 'pity', has been prepared for by the faint irony of 'A paradise for a sect'; and the subdued diction of 'pity these have not' makes an effective entrance for the mellow and peculiarly Keatsian music of

> Traced upon vellum or wild Indian leaf
> The shadows of melodious utterance

which here works vividly to recall the poetic tradition without which, 'bare of laurel' – the classical reference is beautifully in place and evokes no sense of the literary – men 'live, dream and die'. The last line is terse and severe and aptly so after the elaborate euphony of the preceding couplet. The restrained vocabulary and the rhythm broken by repeated implacable pauses increase the feeling of finality and deepen the power of the concluding word. By this point we have felt with intense conviction how the absence of literary tradition reduces the most human acts of the savage and fanatic to meaningless gestures; we have realized how man without it is no more than an unhistorical organism, casual and impermanent. We have also grasped that we are dealing with a major poet and an assured Shakespearean practitioner. 'Shakespearian work it is,' said Arnold; 'not imitative, indeed, of Shakespeare, but Shakespearian, because its expression has that rounded perfection and felicity of loveliness of which Shakespeare is the great master.'[39]

III

Coleridge made a distinction between two classes of writers which helps to illuminate the character of Keats as an artist. It had to do with a mode of imaginative perception with which Shakespeare was endowed and Milton and Wordsworth were not. 'Shakespeare is the Spinozistic deity – an omnipresent creativeness. Milton is the deity of prescience; he stands *ab extra*, and drives a fiery chariot and four, making the horses feel the iron curb which holds them in. Shakespeare's poetry is characterless; that is, it does not reflect the individual Shakespeare; but John Milton himself is in every line of the Paradise lost.'[40] Again he says in *Table Talk*, 'Although Wordsworth and Goethe are not much alike, to be sure, upon the whole; they both have this peculiarity of utter non-sympathy with the subjects of their poetry. They are always, both of them, spectators *ab extra*, – feeling *for*, but never *with*, their characters.' As between these two classes of writers, those who observe from without and those who feel from within, Keats is akin to Shakespeare.

His extraordinary receptiveness to the identity of other things and persons, which I have referred to already, his taking part in the life of the sparrow and the action of the rain, his annihilation in the face of the intrusive presence of others, was at once an immense hospitality towards other forms and modes of being, and a faculty of entering into – not merely comprehending but understanding, as Keats put it[41] – other species, other kinds of lives, otherness itself.

> I feel more and more every day, as my imagination strengthens, that I do not live in this world alone but in a thousand worlds. No sooner am I alone than shapes of epic greatness are stationed around me, and serve my Spirit the office [of] which is equivalent to a King's body guard – then 'Tragedy with scepter'd pall, comes sweeping by.' According to my state of Mind I am with Achilles shouting in the Trenches, or with Theocritus in the Vales of Sicily. Or I throw my whole being into Triolus, and repeating those lines, 'I wander like a lost Soul upon the Stygian Banks staying for waftage', I melt into the air with a voluptuousness so delicate that I am content to be alone.[42]

Keats's imagination leapt over every interval, as he said his mind did in commerce with his friends.[43] It did this all the more in conditions of solitariness, or separation, or distance or opposition. He began, for example, to *understand*, that is, to have a relationship with, so much deeper than mere comprehension of, the cartoons of Raphael, 'By seeing something done in quite an opposite spirit – I mean a picture of Guido's in which all the Saints, instead of that heroic simplicity and unaffected grandeur which they inherit from Raphael, had each of them both in countenance and gesture all the canting, solemn melodramatic mawkishness of MacKenzie's father Nicholas.'[44] The poet, without identity himself, is supremely distinguished by the power of becoming, continually 'informing and filling some other Body'.[45]

To be capable of being informed and filled by the unpoetical chameleon poet, the object had first to possess energy such as we see in the anxious deer, or the purposive stoat, or the balancing hawk, or the wind roaring through the window, or the man quarrelling in the street. Secondly, it had to have intensity, that is, to be part of an activity engaged in with utter absorption and a total lack of self-regard, as with the man hurrying along, his eyes bright with purpose, or the alert concentration instinctive to the deer and the stoat; and thirdly, it had to have beauty, by which Keats meant the potentiality of being seized on by the imagination and thus compelled into reality:

> I am certain of nothing but of the holiness of the Heart's affections and the truth of Imagination – What the imagination seizes as Beauty must be truth – whether it existed before or not – for I have the same Idea of all our Passions as of Love they are all in their sublime, creative of essential Beauty.[46]

Keats, whose lightness of touch never deserted him, could make fun of himself even when he was most seriously probing at the meaning of imagination. He wrote on 16 August 1820 to Shelley, for example, declining an invitation to stay with the Shelleys in Italy, '. . . is not this extraordinary talk for the writer of Endymion? whose mind was like a pack of scattered cards – I am pick'd up and sorted to a pip. My Imagination is a Monastry and I am its Monk – you must explain my metap[hysics] to yourself.'[47] Those metaphysics included the firm conviction that the imagination was a means to discern beauty and to incorporate it with truth in a more inclusive reality. To Keats imagination was the core of experience. Nothing was real until it was experienced and nothing was experienced unless it had been opened by the imagination. Keats would have agreed with Santayana's dictum, 'I have imagination and nothing that is real is alien to me.' When Keats compares the imagination to Adam's dream – 'he awoke and found it truth' – he is directing our attention not only to the terms imagination and truth, but also to 'found'. 'Found it truth' is a phrase which brings home to us the embodying of existence which we find in imagination. Imagination does not simply influence things in the direction of humanity. It succeeds in making them densely and powerfully expressive of human nature. Compared to it other forms of expressiveness are thin and abstract. The imagination embodies both the structure of an experience and its clipped, particular existence, or what Coleridge called both the law of its being and the exact shade of its being. Imagination, unlike consecutive reasoning, as Keats called intellectual analysis, presented the object in all its concrete complexity while simultaneously informing it with that intensity which is the excellence of every art, 'capable of making all disagreeables evaporate, from their being in close relationship with Beauty & Truth . . .'.[48] The disagreeables include, as Bate[49] pointed out, the irrelevant and the discordant which evaporate in the fusion of object and mind. Imagination, which brings intensity to the thing, also makes for disinterestedness in the poet. Without it we should stay gaoled in our private darkness. It breaks down the finitude of personal life and dissipates the illusions of individual selfishness in the interests of a more generous inclusiveness.

When Keats in his letter to Bailey of 22 November 1817 cried out, 'O for a Life of Sensations rather than of Thoughts', he spoke as though these divisions were exhaustive. George Santayana put some of Keats's feelings more lucidly when he wrote, 'between sensation and abstract discourse lies a region of deployed sensibility . . . this region called imagination has pleasures more airy and luminous than those of sense, more massive and rapturous than those of intelligence'. This is the area Keats wishes to inhabit, and this is the sphere which consecutive reasoning cannot bring us to. It belongs to those who delight in sensations – in the wider meaning that Keats, not Santayana, gave the word – rather than those pure intellectuals who hunger after truth like Bailey. It is the pleasures of this part of life, repeated in a finer tone, which Keats speculates make up paradisal happiness, in the same way, indeed, as poetry itself, in its silent working, repeatedly brings back what had been experienced before.

> Adam's dream will do here and seems to be a conviction that Imagination and its empyreal reflection is the same as human Life and its spiritual repetition. But as I was saying – the simple imaginative Mind may have its rewards in the repetition of its own silent Working coming continually on the spirit with a fine suddenness. . . .[50]

If the function of imagination is to multiply possibilities, to endow the elected one with intensity, and then to add to bring it into being, it did not perform this multiple function with equal impartiality among all imagined possibilities. Keats himself described three classes of such things, to which he gave the name ethereal, another example of his personal and independent vocabulary:

> Ethereal thing(s) may at least be thus real, divided under three heads – Things real – things semireal – and no things – Things real – such as existences of Sun Moon & Stars and passages of Shakspeare – Things semireal such as Love, the Clouds &c which require a greeting of the Spirit to make them wholly exist – and Nothings which are made Great and dignified

> by an ardent pursuit – Which by the by stamps the burgundy mark on the bottles of our Minds, insomuch as they are able to '*consec[r]ate whate'er they look upon*'.[51]

Things real have an absolute importance and a totally warranted and objective existence, whereas ambiguities and uncertainties confer only a qualified significance and an intermediate condition upon things semireal, and nothings are purely subjective in their significance. It is the second class of things which, because of its provisional and fleeting existence, requires the greeting of imagination to turn it into rounded reality.

There is a passage in Gerard Manley Hopkins's correspondence with R. W. Dixon which has a striking relevance to Keats's comments on the semireal: 'The world is full of things and events, phenomena of all sorts that go without notice, go unwitnessed. . . . And if we regret this want of witness in brute nature, much more in the things done with lost pains and disappointed hopes by men.'[52] Hopkins's witnessing is like Keats's greeting. To notice an object, even more to greet it, isn't merely to give it recognition but to bring it into existence in a new way. This kind of witnessing and this kind of greeting which endow a thing with a new existence is the creative essence of the art of poetry. It saves part of the miraculous variety of the universe from waste. To witness and to greet in this way is a birth of new life, a release of possibility and an increment to being. It is also, when it is Keats who performs the greeting, a giving of existence with a particular bloom and perfection.

In Keats, then, sensibility starting with a marvellous acuity of the senses, enforced by a profound engagement of the will, and developed through increasing intellectual power and moral energy, advanced by imitation, learning and practice, and was sustained by a continued analysis both of self and art. The completed work was constantly excelled by the attainment of the mind and the personality. The perfection of the one matched the advance of the other only in the final poems.

So far I have discussed Keats's account of the moral, intellectual and imaginative qualities of the producer, the poet, but what about the qualities of the produced, the issue of sensibility, the poetry? The key passage occurs in a letter to John Taylor, written on 27 February 1818:

> In Poetry I have a few Axioms, and you will see how far I am from their Centre. 1st I think Poetry should surprise by a fine excess and not by Singularity – it should strike the Reader as a wording of his own highest thoughts, and appear almost a Remembrance – 2nd Its touches of Beauty should never be half way thereby making the reader breathless instead of content: the rise, the progress, the setting of imagery should be like the Sun come natural natural too him – shine over him and set soberly although in magnificence leaving him in the Luxury of twilight – but it is easier to think what Poetry should be than to write it – and this leads me on to another axiom. That if Poetry comes not as naturally as the Leaves to a tree it had better not come at all.[53]

Keats's first axiom suggests that poetry should achieve its effect by a strong orthodoxy rather than by the arbitrary or eccentric. And the sense by which we recognize in the new a fulfilment of our finest experience, striking the reader as a wording of his own highest thoughts, is very close to the criterion arrived at by Coleridge when considering the development of a standard of musical appreciation: 'I allude,' he said, 'to that sense of recognition which accompanies a sense of novelty in the most original passages of a great composer. If we listen to a symphony of Cimarosa, the present strain still seems not only to recall but almost to revive some past movement, another and yet the same.'[54] The common ground between Coleridge and Keats is a belief in the seamlessness of experience of quality, in the unity of texture between the finest whether familiar or utterly new. The second axiom begins with a characteristically Keatsian intuition, namely, that the reader should be left content rather than breathless, i.e. excited and unsatisfied, by the touches of beauty, and it continues the Coleridge connection[55] in its suggestion that the imagery should also share in this expectedness, naturalness and inevitability, that the imagery, in fact, should in its nature and pacing be acceptable because of the feeling which gives it its tone. And when Keats speaks in the third axiom of poetry coming as naturally as the leaves to a tree or not at all, he seems to me not just, or hardly at all, to be speaking of the ease and fluency of the poet, but rather of the natural organic life of the poem: the word 'comes', I believe, implies the presence – judged to be essential to poetry – of that most inward and unfakeable quality, namely rhythm, and in particular the deep, breathing, biological rhythm of Keats's own poetry.

But the vigorous air of sanity which breathes through everything that Keats wrote in his letters, the powerfully active intellect, and the mature and humorous acceptance of human failing both in himself and others, could not be content with the contemplation and analysis of the individual John Keats and his own particular art and production. He was bound to generalize from his own case to that of the run of mankind, since he saw himself, the artist and poet, as the representative man and the unfolding of his own sensibility as illustrating in a serious way spiritual growth in the rest of mankind. He had his own view and his own highly idiomatic expression of that view, of the way the human soul, as well as its analogue and image, the poetic sensibility, developed and matured. His view was based on the conception of the gap which existed between human potential, the spark of general intelligence on the one hand, and acquired identity, the completed person on the other. This was parallel to the gap which existed between imaginative possibility and the informing actualization of the poetic act. Various elements contributed to the structure by which the gap was crossed: time, the world and human experience were necessities, as were general intelligence, human feeling and painful experience. Circumstances alter nature and, indeed, endow man with a second nature, his human identity.

> Call the world if you Please 'The Vale of Soul-Making' . . . I say '*Soul Making*' Soul as distinguished from an Intelligence – There may be intelligence or sparks of the divinity in millions – but they are not souls till they acquire identities, till each one is personally itself. . . . how then are Souls to be made? . . . How, but by the medium of a world like this? . . . This is effected by three grand materials acting the one upon the other for a series of years – These three materials are the *Intelligence* – the *human heart* (as distinguished from intelligence or Mind) and the *World* or *Elemental Space* suited for the proper action of *Mind and Heart* on each other for the purpose of forming the *Soul* or *Intelligence destined to possess the sense of Identity* . . . I will call the *world* a School instituted for the purpose of teaching little children to read – I will call the *human heart* the *horn Book* used in that School – and I will call the *Child able to read, the Soul* made from that

School and its *hornbook*. Do you not see how necessary a World of Pains and troubles is to school an Intelligence and make it a soul? A Place where the heart must feel and suffer in a thousand diverse ways! Not merely is the Heart a Hornbook, it is the Minds Bible, it is the Minds experience, it is the teat from which the Mind or intelligence sucks its identity – As various as the Lives of men are – so various become their Souls, and thus does God make individual beings, Souls, Identical Souls of the sparks of his own essence . . . I began by seeing how man was formed by circumstances – and what are circumstances? – but touchstones of his heart? – and what are touchstones? – but proovings of his heart? – and what are proovings of his heart but fortifiers or alterers of his nature? and what is his altered nature but his soul? – and what was his soul before it came into the world and had These provings and alterations and perfectionings? – An intelligence(s) – without Identity – and how is this Identity to be made? Through the medium of the heart? And how is the heart to become this Medium but in a world of Circumstance?[56]

Notes

1 *The Use of Imagination* (London: Chatto, 1959).
2 *Letters*, II, p. 360.
3 ibid., I, p. 214.
4 ibid., II, p. 116.
5 ibid., p. 209.
6 ibid., p. 113.
7 ibid., I, p. 271
8 ibid., p. 404.
9 ibid., p. 205.
10 ibid., p. 388.
11 ibid., p. 210.
12 ibid., II, p. 79.
13 ibid., p. 80.
14 ibid., p. 213.
15 ibid., I, p. 277.
16 ibid., p. 279.
17 ibid., p. 277.
18 ibid., p. 243.
19 ibid., p. 232.
20 ibid.
21 ibid., p. 231.
22 ibid., p. 214.
23 ibid.
24 ibid., p. 266.
25 ibid., p. 405.
26 ibid., I, p. 143.
27 ibid., p. 223.
28 ibid., pp. 395–6.
29 ibid., p. 397.
30 ibid., II, p. 101.
31 ibid., I, pp. 280–1.
32 *Little Essays drawn from the Writings of George Santayana*, Logan Pearsall Smith (London: Constable, 1920), p. 125.
33 *Letters*, I, p. 374.
34 ibid.

35 ibid., II, p. 230.
36 Quoted in Bate, *John Keats*, p. 33.
37 Jones, *John Keats's Dream of Truth*, p. 76.
38 F. R. Leavis, *Revaluation* (London: Chatto, 1936), pp. 268–9.
39 *Essays in Criticism*, pp. 120–1.
40 *Table Talk*.
41 *Letters*, II, p. 19.
42 ibid., I, pp. 403–4.
43 Cf. ibid., p. 407.
44 ibid., II, p. 19.
45 ibid., I, p. 387.
46 ibid., p. 184.
47 ibid., II, p. 323.
48 ibid., I, p. 192.
49 Bate, *John Keats*, p. 243.
50 *Letters*, I, p. 185.
51 ibid., pp. 242–3.
52 *The Correspondence of G. M. Hopkins and R. W. Dixon*, ed. C. C. Abbott (London: Oxford University Press, 1935), p. 7
53 *Letters*, I, pp. 238–9.
54 *The Friend*, First Landing-Place I (London: Bell, 1875).
55 Cf. *Biographia Literaria*, XV.
56 *Letters*, II, pp. 102–4.

6
Letters to George and Georgiana

The composition of a soul by the operation of intelligence through the medium of the heart in a world of circumstance: this theme, the analysis of, and Keats's own route to, maturity, the maturity so earnestly laboured after in his life, so lucidly and persuasively theorized about in the letters, is only completely realized in the great art of the Odes and the *Fall of Hyperion*. In these his meditations on maturity, his efforts to achieve it, issue into a disciplined poetic art. Before considering this art, I want to gloss what I have taken to be Keats's definition of the purpose of his art and life, and to pursue it in two sets of letters, the first to George and Georgiana Keats, the second to Fanny Brawne. In the first the emphasis is on 'the provings and alterations and perfectionings' of intelligence; in the second, on 'the medium of the heart'.

In the correspondence I want to look at now, the letters to George and Georgiana Keats sent between 27 June 1818 and 17 January 1820, we discover a more inclusive Keats than the one in his letters to friends, no matter how close, and a fuller personality than the intense, and increasingly pinched, figure to be observed in the letters to Fanny Brawne. We see most clearly the family Keats, and Keats was one to whom the family had shown itself as both a necessary condition of human happiness and psychic health and the frailest structure always liable to collapse. Keats bloomed in the family circle which was his base, cave and spring. In these letters he demonstrates the support and strength it gave him in bearing the anguish of Tom's decline and the capacity, the largeness of spirit, he derived from it, so that he could at the same time welcome with a spontaneous and genuine affection the newest member of the family, Georgiana:

> Our's are ties which independent of their own Sentiment are sent us by providence to prevent the deleterious effects of one great,

> solitary grief. I have Fanny and I have you – three people whose Happiness to me is sacred – and it does annul that selfish sorrow which I should otherwise fall into, living as I do with poor Tom who looks upon me as his only comfort – the tears will come into your Eyes – let them – and embrace each other – thank heaven for what happiness you have and after thinking a moment or two that you suffer in common with all Mankind hold it not a sin to regain your cheerfulness.[1]

Impulses to protect and impulses to welcome balance themselves during this phase in Keats's maturing character. He felt himself related to others through the medium of the family: 'I know not how it is, but I have never made any acquaintance of my own – nearly all through your medium my dear Brother – through you I know not only a Sister but a glorious human being.'[2]

Keats's was a nature that flicked from mood to mood, from grave to light to profound, swiftly and precisely, his feelings being volatile but never blurred. The family with its quick, instinctive accommodation to varieties of character and feeling was the ideal setting for such a temperament, as the letter was its perfect vehicle. Keats manifests precisely that sort of mind described by Lawrence so brilliantly in his remarks about Verga, where he speaks of the mind which makes

> . . . curious swoops and circles. . . . There is a curious spiral rhythm, and the mind approaches again and again the point of concern, repeats itself, goes back, destroys the time-sequence entirely, so that time ceases to exist, as the mind stoops to the quarry, then leaves it without striking, soars, hovers, turns, swoops, stoops again, still does not strike, yet is nearer, nearer, reels away again, wheels off into the air, even forgets, quite forgets, yet again turns, bends, circles slowly, swoops and stoops again, until at last there is the closing-in, and the clutch of a decision or a resolve.[3]

All Keats's letters illustrate this swerving, circling habit. But even if I confine myself to a single letter, that written between 14 and 31 October 1818, that will provide more than enough for a demonstration. I should point out that Keats made this observation about himself. He speaks of 'the activity of my Mind; of its inability to remain at rest'.[4] In the space of this long letter we see the straightforward Keats gaining 'so much pleasure from the simple idea of [his brother's] playing a game at cricket'.[5] We see the practical and domestic Keats worried about his sister, working on her reluctant guardian to get her to visit Hampstead, and stoically suffering with his dying brother. Tom was always edging his way into consciousness, whatever Keats was speaking of: 'On Thursday I walked with Hazlitt as far as covent Garden: he was going to play Rackets – I think Tom has been rather better these few last days – he has been less nervous.'[6] There is a Verga-like logic in following the athletic Hazlitt with the invalid Tom. Again in the same letter we see the Keats who delighted in women. It is in this letter that he described Jane Cox, a woman for whom he felt an admiring sensuality though no pang of real feeling. Thinking of her enforces his belief in his own independence:

> Though the most beautiful Creature were waiting for me at the end of a Journey or a Walk; though the carpet were of Silk, the Curtains of the morning Clouds; the chairs and Sofa stuffed with Cygnet's down; the food Manna, the Wine beyond Claret, the Window opening on Winander mere, I should not feel – or rather my Happiness would not be so fine, as my Solitude is sublime. Then instead of what I have described, there is a Sublimity to welcome me home – The roaring of the wind is my wife and the Stars through the window pane are my Children. The mighty abstract Idea I have of Beauty in all things stifles the more divided and minute domestic happiness – an amiable wife and sweet Children I contemplate as a part of that Beauty, but I must have a thousand of those beautiful particles to fill up my heart. I feel more and more every day, as my imagination strengthens, that I do not live in this world alone but in a thousand worlds.[7]

He goes on to remark that not only his imaginative life but also his opinions of the generality of women, to whom, he adds absurdly, he would rather give a sugar plum than his time, 'form a barrier against Matrimony which I rejoice in'.[8] There is plenty of gossip in this letter, some feminine and bitchy, for example, about the Miss Reynoldses, who had displeased him – 'Now I am coming[9] the Richardson,' he says self-mockingly – some robustly comic. 'There was a downright Scotchman' – on the boat coming back from Inverness to London – 'who hearing that there had been a bad crop of Potatoes in England had brought some triumphant Specimens from Scotland – these he exhibited with national pride to all the Lightermen, and Watermen from the Nore to the Bridge.'[10] We see the social Keats leading a remarkably active life, visiting his friends, going to the opera. 'I have been but once to Haydon's, once to Hunt's, once to Rice's, once to Hessey's, I have not seen Taylor, I have not been to the Theatre.'[11] There is also the patriotic and political Keats, one like Coleridge for whom politics was, or ought to be, a form of moral activity:

> There is of a truth nothing manly or sterling in any part of the Government. There are many Madmen In the Country, I have no doubt, who would like to be beheaded on tower Hill merely for the sake of eclat, there are many Men like Hunt who from a principle of taste would like to see things go on better, there are many like Sir F. Burdett who like to sit at the head of political dinners – but there are none prepared to suffer in obscurity for their Country – the motives of our worst Men are interest and of our best Vanity – we have no Milton, no Algernon Sidney – Governors in these days loose the title of Man in exchange for that of Diplomat and Minister – We breathe in a sort of Official Atmosphere – all the departments of Government have strayed far from Simplicity which is the greatest of Strength – there is as much difference in this respect between the present Government and Oliver Cromwell's, as there is between the 12 Tables of Rome and the volumes of Civil Law which were digested by Justinian. A Man now entitled Chancellor has the same honour paid to him whether he be a Hog or a Lord Bacon. No sensation is created by Greatness but by the number of orders a Man has at his Button holes Notwithstand the part which the Liberals take in the Cause of Napoleon I cannot but think he has done more harm to the life of Liberty than any one else could have done: not that the divine right Gentlemen have done or intend to do any good – no they have taken a Lesson of him and will do all the further harm he would have done without any of the good – The worst thing he has done is, that he has taught them how to organize their monstrous armies.[12]

There is also, of course, the poet who is both self-deprecating and profoundly aware of his own powers. A practising poet has to concern himself not only with creative activity but also with the practical business of placing and publishing his work as well as the reactions of critics and the public to it. We see both sides of the poet's life in this letter. Reynolds, he reports, is persuading him to publish 'A Pot of Basil' as an answer to the attacks made on him in *Blackwood's Magazine* and the *Quarterly Review*. He notes the two letters published in his defence in the *Chronicle* and the one in the *Examiner*, a letter written by Reynolds and reprinted from a West of England paper. He notices how the attempt to crush him in the *Quarterly* has only brought him into more notice, and 'it is a common expression among book men "I wonder the Quarterly should cut its own throat"'.[13] He finds himself disturbed by a ferment of inward activity. He speaks of sending George and Georgiana a story – 'It must be prose and not very exciting'[14] – which he will write to quieten his disturbed mind. The one thing, he remarks, that ever affected him personally for more than one short passing day, is doubt about his powers for poetry, 'I seldom have any, and I look with hope to the nighing time when I shall have none.'[15] He is indifferent to what people think of him: 'Some think me middling, others silly, others foolish – every one thinks he sees my weak side against my will; when in truth it is with my will – I am content to be thought all this because I have in my own breast so great a resource.'[16]

To protect, to increase, and to understand this inner resource was the motive powerfully working through this phase of Keats's life, say from the summer of 1818 to the winter of 1819. It was a motive derived from a positive and profound sense of his own powers. 'I think I shall be among the English Poets after my death,'[17] he announces to his brother and sister-in-law with a restrained but strong assurance. Part of that assurance was an unusual confidence, both intellectual and emotional, about disinterestedness, value and standard, the 'mighty abstract Idea I have of Beauty in all things',[18] as he puts it, or 'the yearning Passion I have for the beautiful'.[19] It was his confidence about this order of reality that turned him against those like Hunt who seemed incapable of grasping the sureness of Keats's possession or unaware of it altogether, or insensitively patronizing about it:

> Hunt – who is certainly a pleasant fellow in the main when you are with him – but in reality he is vain, egotistical and disgusting in matters of taste and in morals. – He understands many a beautiful thing; but then, instead of giving other minds credit for the same degree of perception as he himself possesses – he begins an explanation in such a curious manner that our taste and self-love

> is offended continually. Hunt does one harm by making fine things petty and beautiful things hateful – Through him I am indifferent to Mozart, I care not for white Busts – and many a glorious thing when associated with him becomes a nothing – This distorts one's mind – makes one's thoughts bizarre – perplexes one in the standard of Beauty.[20]

It may be that this severe judgement of Hunt, who never varied in his appreciation of Keats, may be exaggerated and unfair, but the essential point Keats is making is a most significant one in itself and for his development. He repeats more than once that his modesty about other parts of his life must not be thought to imply any lack of certainty on his part in matters of literary taste, 'I never can feel certain of any truth but from a clear perception of its Beauty – and I find myself very young minded even in that perceptive power – which I hope will increase.'[21] He sees it increasing daily. Raphael's cartoons, baffling a year ago, he now begins to understand. No doubt it was some sense he had of a corresponding force and clarity of conviction in Hazlitt which led him so to approve of Hazlitt's lectures, from which he quoted extensively in his letters to the George Keatses. It was this confidence too about standards, even more than his own treatment by them, which made him despise the contemporary reviews. They

> have enervated and made indolent men's minds – few think for themselves – These Reviews too are getting more and more powerful and especially the Quarterly – They are like a superstition which the more it prostrates the Crowd and the longer it continues the more powerful it becomes just in proportion to their increasing weakness – I was in hopes that when people saw, as they must do now, all the trickery and iniquity of these Plagues they would scout them, but no they are like the spectators at the Westminster cock-pit – they like the battle and do not care who wins or who looses.[22]

The disabling process which Keats variously described as enervating the mind or perplexing one in the standard of beauty was not solely the result of external influences like bad criticism or the ill judgement of friends. There were also internal reasons, and particularly was this so in Keats's own case. Continually in the letters and in the poetry, we see the history of the friction of two elements in Keats's nature: on the one hand, the qualities of intensity and concentration, on the other an infatuation with the drowsily vague and the languorously narcotic. Keats, one hardly needs to make the claim, was an artist of the most distinguished intellectual powers. Having, as his letters abundantly corroborate, precisely that 'swift, strangely sovereign and anticipatory grasp and assimilation as sure as easy',[23] which Thomas Mann specified as the character of intellectual genius, he saw, better than any friend or critic, and more discerningly than any who have come after him, how his nature was moved in two opposed ways. Sometimes he described this conflict as one between energy and passivity, or between dreamy contemplation and imaginative activity. He made the distinction very clear in the following words:

> On Sunday I went to Davenports' where I dined – and had a nap. I cannot bear a day annihilated in that manner – there is a great difference between an easy and an uneasy indolence – An indolent day – fill'd with speculations even of an unpleasant colour – is bearable and even pleasant alone – when one's thoughts cannot find out any thing better in the world; and experience has told us that locomotion is no change: but to have nothing to do, and to be surrounded with unpleasant human identities; who press upon one just enough to prevent one getting into a lazy position; and not enough to interest or rouse one; is a capital punishment of a capital crime; for is not giving up, through good nature, one's time to people who have no light and shade a capital crime? Yet what can I do? – they have been very kind and attentive to me.[24]

(How characteristic, by the way, of Keats's temperament that he should expose himself to this kind of maddening irritation because people had been kind and affectionate to him. It is easy to overlook this homely, cobbled quality, this touch of domestic sweetness, in a genius preoccupied with some of the most profound themes in life and art. It is impossible to exaggerate the simple, human niceness of Keats.)

The paradox of Keats's nature, a cluster of contraries, can be vividly illustrated in the part of a letter he wrote on Friday 19 March 1819, which begins with a rueful anecdote about being banged in the eye with a cricket ball, for the second time since he left school, and then goes on to show first, that special combination of electric mental vitality and lax, indulgent emotion; it continues with astonishingly contrasting passages of self-intoxication on the one hand and powerful philosophic discernment on the other. Phrases and sentences of this letter, one of Keats's greatest, will appear more than once in this study, but it seems to me to give so total a portrait of every aspect of his genius that I quote it in full.

> Yesterday I got a black eye – the first time I took a Cricket bat – Brown who is always one's friend in a disaster applied a leech to the eyelid, and there is no inflammation this morning though the ball hit me directly on the sight – 't was a white ball – I am glad it was not a clout – This is the second black eye I have had since leaving school – during all my school days I never had one at all – we must eat a peck before we die – This morning I am in a sort of temper indolent and supremely careless: I long after a stanza or two of Thompson's Castle of indolence – My passions are all asleep from my having slumbered till nearly eleven and weakened the animal fibre all over me to a delightful sensation about three degrees on this side of faintness – if I had teeth of pearl and the breath of lillies I should call it languor – but as I am* I must call it Laziness – In this state of effeminacy the fibres of the brain are relaxed in common with the rest of the body, and to such a happy degree that pleasure has no show of enticement and pain no unbearable frown. Neither Poetry, nor ambition, nor Love have any alertness of countenance as they pass by me; they seem rather like three figures on a greek vase – a Man and two women – whom no one but myself could distinguish in their disguisement. This is the only happiness; and is a rare instance of advantage in the body overpowering the Mind. I have this moment received a note from Haslam in which he expects the death of his Father who has been for some time in a state of insensibility – his mother bears up he says very well – I shall go to town tomorrow to see him. This is the world – thus we cannot expect to give way many hours to pleasure – Circumstances are like Clouds continually gathering and bursting – While we are laughing the seed of some trouble is put into the wide arable land of events – while we are laughing it sprouts it grows and suddenly bears a poison fruit which we must pluck – Even so we have leisure to reason on the misfortunes of our friends; our own

* especially as I have a black eye

touch us too nearly for words. Very few men have ever arrived at a complete disinterestedness of Mind: very few have been influenced by a pure desire of the benefit of others – in the greater part of the Benefactors (of) & to Humanity some meretricious motive has sullied their greatness – some melodramatic scenery has fascinated them – From the manner in which I feel Haslam's misfortune I perceive how far I am from any humble standard of disinterestedness – Yet this feeling ought to be carried to its highest pitch, as there is no fear of its ever injuring society – which it would do I fear pushed to an extremity – For in wild nature the Hawk would loose his Breakfast of Robins and the Robin his of Worms The Lion must starve as well as the swallow – The greater part of Men make their way with the same instinctiveness, the same unwandering eye from their purposes, the same animal eagerness as the Hawk – The Hawk wants a Mate, so does the Man – look at them both they set about it and procure one in the same manner – They want both a nest and they both set about one in the same manner – they get their food in the same manner – The noble animal Man for his amusement smokes his pipe – the Hawk balances about the Clouds – that is the only difference of their leisures. This it is that makes the Amusement of Life – to a speculative Mind. I go among the Fields and catch a glimpse of a stoat or a fieldmouse peeping out of the withered grass – the creature hath a purpose and its eyes are bright with it – I go amongst the buildings of a city and I see a Man hurrying along – to what? The Creature has a purpose and his eyes are bright with it. But then as Wordsworth says, 'we have all one human heart' – there is an electric fire in human nature tending to purify – so that among these human creatures there is continually some birth of new heroism – The pity is that we must wonder at it: as we should at finding a pearl in rubbish – I have no doubt that thousands of People never heard of have had hearts completely disinterested: I can remember but two – Socrates and Jesus – their Histories evince it – What I heard a little time ago, Taylor observes with respect to Socrates, may be said of Jesus – That he was so great a man that though he transmitted no writing of his own to posterity, we have his Mind and his sayings and his greatness handed to us by others. It is to be lamented that the history of the latter was written and revised by

Men interested in the pious frauds of Religion. Yet through all this I see his splendour. Even here though I myself am pursuing the same instinctive course as the veriest human animal you can think of – I am however young writing at random – straining at particles of light in the midst of a great darkness – without knowing the bearing of any one assertion of any one opinion. Yet may I not in this be free from sin? May there not be superior beings amused with any graceful, though instinctive attitude my mind may fall into, as I am entertained with the alterness of a Stoat or the anxiety of a Deer? Though a quarrel in the streets is a thing to be hated, the energies displayed in it are fine; the commonest Man shows a grace in his quarrel – By a superior being our reasoning[s] may take the same tone – though erroneous they may be fine – This is the very thing in which consists poetry; and if so it is not so fine a thing as philosophy – For the same reason that an eagle is not so fine a thing as a truth – Give me this credit – Do you not think I strive – to know myself? Give me this credit – and you will not think that on my own account I repeat Milton's lines

> 'How charming is divine Philosophy
> Not harsh and crabbed as dull fools suppose
> But musical as is Apollo's lute' –

No – not for myself – feeling grateful as I do to have got into a state of mind to relish them properly – Nothing ever becomes real till it is experienced – Even a Proverb is no proverb to you till your Life has illustrated it – I am ever afraid that your anxiety for me will lead you to fear for the violence of my temperament continually smothered down: for that reason I did not intend to have sent you the following sonnet [the sonnet beginning 'Why did I laugh tonight? No voice will tell'] – but look over the two last pages and ask yourselves whether I have not that in me which will bear the buffets of the world.[25]

The importance of this extraordinary statement is that it gives immediate access to the operations of a mind at once strenuous, subtle and profound, in which every movement is touched with a passionate individuality and which is – the other side of Keats's too-narrow and defective professional education – saved both by personality and experience from any conventional position or passively orthodox logic. Even if we do no more than enumerate the topics alluded to we shall have a notion of the range of Keats's mind. He glides – I use the word to indicate the smoothness of movement not to hint at any superficiality – from cricket to indolence, and to attempting to define and distinguish the double character of his fascination with it, i.e. that it could be active as well as passive – a fact that his phrase 'if I had teeth of pearl and the breath of lillies I should call it languor' makes evident. The general terms 'pleasure' and 'pain' lead him, with his appetite for the particular, to personify, and mysterious figures of poetry, ambition and life pass before him, personified but without identity. At this point indolence becomes serenity, the body overpowers the mind, the mind articulates the physical sensations. From this rare species of contemplation he moves with precise but fleeting logic to a specific instance of the other, ravaged side of human experience, the sadness called up by the note from Haslam about the imminent death of his father. Then with a smooth and natural turn, he goes from the concrete back to the general. His generalization is, of course, a Keatsian one, that is, terms that are figurative and solid – 'Circumstances are like Clouds continually gathering and bursting – While we are laughing the seed of some trouble is put into the wide arable land of events – while we are laughing it sprouts it grows and suddenly bears a poison fruit which we must pluck.' In these words he describes both a particular state of mind and a general theory of life – one directly opposite to that held by the Godwin-perfectibility men. But the tragedy of life is not responded to by men with a corresponding disinterestedness. There is invariably in men's reaction something meretricious or vain or cheap, as he confesses he observes in himself.

But disinterestedness (carried to its highest pitch) is for him the highest value of life, present in the operations of nature as in the unreflecting actions of men. The magnificence of life, and the splendour of art, are both to be found in this untainted, absolute energy of disinterestedness. From this vitality comes every triumph of life, every supreme achievement, every singularity of genius. Its perfect figures are Socrates and Jesus. Keats can still discern amid the pious frauds of religion the genuine splendour. He acknowledges how hard he has to strain for light in this baffling gloom. He feels blindfolded by the limitations of his own insight but there may be, he reflects, a superior being capable of valuing man's partial energies in the way that the human individual appreciates them in the animals. We see Keats here acknowledging what Santayana claimed about the life of the mind, that it can be as passionate as sense: 'The life of theory is not less human or less emotional than the life of sense; it is more typically human and more keenly emotional. . . . To object to theory in poetry would be like objecting to words there.'[26] At the same time Keats expresses the profound conviction gained in all his laborious efforts to know himself, that nothing is real until it is experienced. A life in this sense is the concrete illustration of truth and the greatest lives are the most figurative. Throughout this astonishing passage we are indeed aware of immense intellectual force, a potent and creative energy, and we feel sympathetic to Keats's description of the violence of his temperament which has to be continually smothered down. Certainly the letter confirms the existence of that inner resource which he claims will enable him 'to bear the buffets of the world'.

Keats's remark about the violence of his temperament comes from one endowed with a quite unusual clarity of self-discernment. He was intimately conscious of his own nature but never, or hardly ever, histrionic or blurred in the accuracy of his reporting of it. What he took to be violence, therefore, almost certainly was. To the reader, however, it seems, certainly in its results, more like a gift for intensity, a compressed, piercing power capable of investing impressions with a palpable solidity, of conducting thought at extreme pressure, and of investing moral judgements with a moving force. There is activity, if not violence, even in Keats's moods of self-indulgence, deliciously-tasting melancholy, even in his swooning escapist play with the idea of death. Keats was well aware that some of his speculations about life and art, just like some of his probings into his own character, were hectic and disorderly, distorted both by his personal situation and his lack of knowledge. His aim, his quite deliberate aim, was to educate himself towards a firmer, more philosphic tranquillity, 'a more thoughtful and quiet power. I am more frequently, now, contented to read and think – but now & then, haunted with ambitious thoughts. Quieter in my pulse, improved in my digestion; exerting myself against vexing speculations – scarcely content to write the best verses for the fever they leave behind. I want to compose without this fever.'[27]

The means he chose to this end were orthodox and traditional. It did occur to him that what he needed was an expansion of his 'experience', as many a young modern writer would certainly have felt.

Keats wished to increase his knowledge and to train his mind by learning more. He makes mention, when speaking of his current reading of Ariosto, of his concern to make his Italian equal to his French. He is even willing to take up Church history. He wants to develop a better grounded and keener historical sense:

> We with our bodily eyes see but the fashion and Manners of one country for one age – and then we die – Now to me manners and customs long since passed whether among the Babylonians or the Bactrians are as real, or even more real than those among which I now live – My thoughts have turned lately this way – The more we know the more inadequacy we discover in the world to satisfy us – this is an old observation – but I have made up my Mind never to take any thing for granted – but even to examine the truth of the commonest proverbs:[28]

To develop, that is, at one and the same time a historical sense and to test it by his own experience. Moreover, he wishes to bring a new flow of critical intelligence into his art. A particular exemplification of this is his clear rejection of unsatisfactory models. Spenser is given up for Milton, and Milton only reinforces his deep conviction of the essential influence of Shakespeare. Dante he has found a productive influence but Keats is determined never to become so attached to a foreign idiom as to bring it into his own work. The phrase 'foreign idiom' immediately brings Milton to his mind:

> The Paradise Lost though so fine in itself is a corruption of our Language – it should be kept as it is unique – a curiosity, a beautiful and grand Curiosity. The most remarkable Production of the world – A northern dialect accommodating itself to greek and latin inversions and intonations. The purest English I think – or what ought to be the purest – is Chatterton's – the Language had existed long enough to be entirely uncorrupted of Chaucer's gallicisms and still the old words are used – Chatterton's language is entirely northern – I prefer the native music of it to Milton's cut by feet I have but lately stood on my guard against Milton. Life to him would be death to me. Miltonic verse cannot be written but in the vein of art – I wish to devote myself to another sensation.[29]

The view of life which the maturing Keats came to have as a result of these efforts at self-education was for all its Romantic fervour essentially classical and tragic. On the one hand he appreciated the splendour of man's achievement, on the other he sees man as limited and flawed. His attitude was neither facile nor optimistic nor rigid and obscurantist. It was at once passionate and sceptical, appreciative and disenchanted. It is the attitude Santayana described as 'hopeful without illusion and independent without rebellion'. He could not accept a straightforward religious or Christian expression of history and the nature of man as seen from this point of view. His own formulation comes from the great letter of 21 April, and I give the first part of his statement (the second I have referred to elsewhere).

> I have been reading lately two very different books Robertson's America and Voltaire's Siecle De Louis xiv. It is like walking arm and arm between Pizarro and the great-little Monarch. In How lamentable a case do we see the great body of the people in both instances: in the first, where Men might seem to inherit quiet of Mind from unsophisticated senses; from uncontamination of civilisation; and especially from their being as it were estranged from the mutual helps of Society and its mutual injuries – and thereby more immediately under the Protection of Providence – even there they had mortal pains to bear as bad; or even worse than Baliffs, Debts and Poverties of civilised Life – The whole appears to resolve into this – that Man is originally 'a poor forked creature' subject to the same mischanses as the beasts of the forest, destined to hardships and disquietude of some kind or other. If he improves by degrees his bodily accommodations and comforts – at each stage, at each accent there are waiting for him a fresh set of annoyances – he is mortal and there is still a heaven with its Stars above his head. The most interesting question that can come before us is, How far by the persevering endeavours of a seldom appearing Socrates Mankind may be made happy – I can imagine such happiness carried to an extreme – but what must it end in? – Death – and who could in such a case bear with death – the whole troubles of life which are now frittered away in a series of years, would then be accumulated for the last days of a being who instead of hailing its approach, would leave this world as Eve left Paradise – But in truth I do not at all believe in this

> sort of perfectibility – the nature of the world will not admit of it – the inhabitants of the world will correspond to itself – Let the fish philosophise the ice away from the Rivers in winter time and they shall be at continual play in the tepid delight of Summer. Look at the Poles and at the sands of Africa, Whirlpools and volcanoes – Let man exterminate them and I will say that they may arrive at earthly Happiness – The point at which Man may arrive is as far as the parallel state in inanimate nature and no further – For instance suppose a rose to have sensation, it blooms on a beautiful morning it enjoys itself – but there comes a cold wind, a hot sun – it can not escape it, it cannot destroy its annoyances – they are as native to the world as itself: no more can man be happy in spite, the worldly elements will prey upon his nature – the Common cognomen of this world among the misguided and superstitious is 'a vale of tears' from which we are to be redeemed by a certain arbitrary interposition of God and taken to Heaven – What a little circumscribed straightened notion! Call the world if you Please 'The vale of Soul-making'.[30]

Keats came from a lower-middle-class background which knew poverty although it was connected with means, and he lived in a literary and artistic setting. He derived from the former and kept up amid the latter modest Regency tastes for girls (though he was awkward in company), cards (which he could play all night on occasion), and claret, which he loved 'to a degree' and on which he could write more lyrically than any wine columnist: 'For really 't is so fine – it fills the mouth one's mouth with a gushing freshness – then goes down cool and feverless – then you do not feel it quarrelling with your liver – no it is rather a Peace maker and lies as quiet as it did in the grape.'[31] He liked what one thinks of as Regency food: 'I said this same Claret is the only palate-passion I have I forgot game I must plead guilty to the breast of a Partridge, the back of a hare, the backbone of a grouse, the wing and side of a Pheasant and a Woodcock *passim*.'[32] He was physically strong before his disease took hold of him, capable of walking many hard miles when on his travels in Scotland, or tramping, for example, in London from Westminster to Highgate as a fairly routine outing. The only symptom of weakness he showed was a chronic sore throat which is mentioned with sinister regularity. He made constant fun of himself and unmalicious fun of others. Here, for example, is a set of questions addressed to Georgiana about life in the settlement:

> Now you have by this time crumpled up your large Bonnet, what do you wear – a cap! do you put your hair in papers of a night? do you pay the Miss Birkbeck's a morning visit – have you any tea? or do you milk and water with them – what place of Worship do you go to – the Quakers the Moravians, the Unitarians or the Methodists – Are there any flowers in bloom you like – any beautiful heaths – Any Streets full of Corset Makers. What sort of shoes have you to fit those pretty feet of yours? Do you desire comp[limen]ts to one another? Do you ride on Horseback? What do you have for breakfast, dinner and supper? without mentioning lunch and bever and wet and snack – and a bit to stay one's stomach – Do you get any spirits – now you might easily distil some whiskey – and going into the woods set up a whiskey shop for the Monkeys – Do you and the Miss Birkbecks get groggy on any thing.[33]

He did not regard himself as a sensual person in spite of his liking for claret and food and women's company. He was used to the privations, he maintained, and in the midst of the world lived like a hermit. His hermitical periods were punctured by some intense social activity, however. He was not ignorant of his reputation and of what would be required to improve it. He wrote on 17 September about his proposed tragedy for Kean, 'My name with the literary fashionables is vulgar – I am a weaver boy to them – a Tragedy would lift me out of this mess. And mess it is as far as it regards our Pockets.'[34] He offers his brother advice, suggesting that he might learn from what he does when he is low:

> But be not cast down any more than I am. I feel I can bear real ills better than imaginary ones. Whenever I find myself growing vapourish, I rouse myself, wash and put on a clean shirt brush my hair and clothes, tie my shoestrings neatly and in fact adonize as I were going out – then all clean and comfortable I sit down to write.[35]

And while he could be irritated by external things, for example, the postman Bentley's boys and their racket when he lodged with them, 'Their little voices are like wasps stings',[36] his greatest irritation was caused by unmanly or undignified behaviour. He was disgusted with Dilke who was an anxious and officious parent, entirely swallowed up in his boy, suffering for his every bruise: 'The boy has nothing in his ears all day but himself. . . . O what a farce is our greatest cares!'[37]

He had a sharp gift of observation, although he claimed to dislike description and complained that it took very many words to communicate the identity of something that one could explain in a moment face to face. This skill in notation extended to action, to place, to others, and to himself. He speaks, for example, of the peasants in Scotland handling his companion Brown's spectacles 'as we do a sensitive leaf'.[38] Here again is his bold and energetic sketch of Fingal's cave:

> The finest thing is Fingal's cave: it is entirely a breaking away of basalt pillars. Suppose now the Giants, who came down to the daughters of Men, had taken a whole mass of these Columns and bound them together like Bunches of Matches; and then with immense axes had made a Cavern in the body of these Columns. Such is Fingal's cave except that the sea has done this work of excavation and is continually dashing there.[39]

Or, in another and more comic idiom, this is how he remembers the side streets in Winchester:

> The side-streets here are excessively maiden lady like – The door steps always fresh from the flannel. The knockers have a very staid serious, nay almost quietness about them – I never saw so quiet a collection of Lions, and rams heads.[40]

Here is his view of the tedious Mrs Millar:

> Mrs Millar began a long story and you know it is her Daughter's way to help her on as though her tongue were ill of the gout – Mrs M. certainly tells a Story as though she had been taught her Alphabet in Crutched Friars.[41]

Better still, for its lightness of touch and slight sending-up of self, is the cool sketch of himself writing:

> . . . for the candles are burnt down and I am using the wax taper – which has a long snuff on it – the fire is at its last click – I am sitting with my back to it with one foot rather askew upon the rug and the other with the heel a little elevated from the carpet.[42]

He was always, indeed, strongly affected by his visual sense. He complained about parties where there was no woman worth looking at: 'let my eyes be fed or I'll never go out to dinner any where.'[43]

The light-hearted, bantering, gossipy Keats to be observed throughout this correspondence, even in the concluding letter written to Georgiana alone between 13 and 28 January 1820 (her husband being absent from her, mending his financial fences in London), is, one cannot help noting, sometimes attended by another Keats. I do not mean the ecstatic, fainting aesthete, but an altogether grimmer presence, stricken not only with the tragic but the pointless in human life. It shows itself on the one hand in *accidie*, as when he writes to Georgiana meaning to comfort her in her isolation by referring to his own:

> 'T is best to remain aloof from people and like their good parts without being eternally troubled with the dull processes of their every day Lives. When once a person has smok'd the vapidness of the routine of Society he must have either self interest or the love of some sort of distinction to keep him in good humour with it. All I can say is that standing at Charing Cross and looking east west north and south I can see nothing but dullness.[44]

Moreover, Keats's sense of the tedium of life was not alleviated by any religious consolation. Not that Keats was positively irreligious (he accepted, he said after Tom's death, some kind of immortality), although he was certainly anti-clerical: 'I begin to hate Parsons – they did not make me love them that day – when I saw them in their proper colours – A Parson is a Lamb in a drawing room and a lion in a Vestry.'[45] He was one who drew more from the classical than the biblical myth, more from Lemprière's *Classical Dictionary* and Tooke's *Pantheon* than from the Bible. The other side of his recognition of the harshness of life was his heightened sense of change. Distance and loneliness brought home to him the fact of change and the manner in which change could render people and oneself unrecognizable and totally other:

> From the time you left me, our friends say I have altered completely – am not the same person – perhaps in this letter I am for in a letter one takes up one's existence from the time we last met – I dare say you have altered also – every man does – Our bodies every seven years are completely fresh-materiald – seven

> years ago it was not this hand that clench'd itself against Hammond – We are like the relict garments of a Saint: the same and not the same: for the careful Monks patch it and patch it: till there's not a thread of the original garment left, and still they show it for St Anthony's shirt. This is the reason why men who had been bosom friends, on being separated for any number of years, afterwards meet coldly, neither of them knowing why – The fact is they are both altered – Men who live together have a silent moulding and influencing power over each other – They interassimulate. 'T is an uneasy thought that in seven years the same hands cannot greet each other again.[46]

Change as Keats conceived it carried no poetic murmuration, no plangency of *lacrimae rerum*. Instead it was cold, medical, conclusive. The one way out of the change and unease of life was, Keats affirmed, 'by a willful and dramatic exercise of our Minds towards each other'.[47] Certainly the principal personal relationship of the remaining year and a half of Keats's life vividly illustrates these characteristics of 'willfulness' and 'drama', in pretty well every sense that we can give these terms.

Notes

1 *Letters*, I, pp. 391–2.
2 ibid., p. 392.
3 *D. H. Lawrence, Selected Literary Criticism*, ed. Anthony Beal (London: Heinemann, 1955), p. 290.
4 *Letters*, I, p. 401.
5 ibid., p. 392.
6 ibid., p. 402
7 ibid., p. 403.
8 ibid., p. 404.
9 Both W. J. Bate and H. E. Rollins surprise one in finding this old London idiom (cf. 'coming the old acid') puzzling.
10 *Letters*, I, p. 393.
11 ibid., p. 400.
12 ibid., pp. 396–7.
13 ibid., p. 394.
14 ibid., p. 401.
15 ibid., p. 404.
16 ibid.
17 ibid., p. 394.
18 ibid., p. 403.
19 ibid., p. 404.
20 ibid., II, p. 11.
21 ibid., p. 19.
22 ibid., p. 65.
23 Thomas Mann, *Doctor Faustus* (Harmondsworth: Penguin, 1968), p. 36.
24 *Letters*, II, p. 77.
25 ibid., pp. 78–81.
26 George Santayana, *Three Philosophical Poets* (Cambridge, Mass.: Harvard University Press, 1941), p. 142.

27 *Letters*, II, p. 209.
28 ibid., p. 18.
29 ibid., p. 212.
30 ibid., pp. 100–2.
31 ibid., p. 64.
32 ibid., pp. 64–5.
33 ibid., p. 92.
34 ibid., p. 186.
35 ibid.
36 ibid., p. 90.
37 ibid., pp. 84–5.
38 ibid., p. 197.
39 ibid., p. 198.
40 ibid., p. 201.
41 ibid., I, p. 393.
42 ibid., II, p. 73.
43 ibid., p. 20.
44 ibid., p. 244.
45 ibid., p. 63.
46 ibid., pp. 208–9.
47 ibid., p. 209.

7
Letters to Fanny Brawne

Keats's extant letters to Fanny Brawne begin in July 1819. In May he had written the odes 'On a Grecian Urn', 'A Nightingale', 'Melancholy', 'Indolence'. Thus the correspondence opens in a period of great creative achievement. We possess only Keats's side of the correspondence, and so we must guess at Fanny's reaction and riposte. But from what is implied in Keats's letters, as well as from the existing letters of Fanny Brawne to Keats's sister Fanny, we can tell that her part of the correspondence is crisper, more practical, and by no means limp or submissive. She was not afraid to complain to Keats about the malicious behaviour of some of his friends towards her. Young as she was, Fanny had a quality of steadiness and independence. It is clear that she would not be bullied or emotionally blackmailed, or wholly put down even by Keats. Moreover, while her love, in keeping with her cooler, more limited nature, was less profound and racking than Keats's, there is no reason whatever to suppose that she hadn't a genuine affection for the poet, nor that she was at all insensitive to his tragic situation. She refused to break off the engagement. She helped to nurse him in her mother's house. Clearly she had the interests of a young girl – she was eighteen – and she could not wholly subordinate these to Keats's increasingly jealous suspicions.

Even the first letter, written from Shanklin on 1 July 1819, touches a note which is to become persistent, namely the association of love and death. Night, darkness, silence, in some ways appropriate conditions of love, imply in Keats's mind their other context, the grave:

> The morning is the only proper time for me to write to a beautiful Girl whom I love so much: for at night, when the lonely day has closed, and the lonely, silent, unmusical Chamber is waiting to receive me as into a Sepulchre, then believe me my passion gets

> entirely the sway, then I would not have you see those Rapsodies which I once thought it impossible I should ever give way to, and which I have often laughed at in another, for fear you should [think me] either too unhappy or perhaps a little mad.[1]

Keats is in a state in which moments of rapture never exist absolutely in themselves but carry in their train contrasting memories:

> I have never known any unalloy'd Happiness for many days together: the death or sickness of some one has always spoilt my hours – and now when none such troubles oppress me, it is you must confess very hard that another sort of pain should haunt me. Ask yourself my love whether you are not very cruel to have so entrammelled me, so destroyed my freedom.[2]

There reappears also in these letters that drowning feeling or that attraction towards oblivion which belongs to the softer, less potent part of Keats's nature. It was a motive of his constantly making love a form of intoxication or drug. Almost from the beginning, too, his uneasiness with women which now takes the form of jealousy, also makes its presence felt:

> . . . I shall still love you – but what hatred shall I have for another! Some lines I read the other day are continually ringing a peal in my ears:
>
> To see those eyes I prize above mine own
> Dart favors on another –
> And those sweet lips (yielding immortal nectar)
> Be gently press'd by any but myself –
> Think, think Francesca, what a cursed thing
> It were beyond expression![3]

A week later we hear again his feeling of love as 'that luxurious power over my senses',[4] a heightened but unthinking state which he contrasts with 'that dull sort of patience that cannot be called Life'.[5] Love is 'fire . . . moistened and bedewed with Pleasures'.[6] Fanny, at more than one point during this correspondence, must have rebuked Keats for his concentration on her beauty – usually spelt by Keats with a capital in his own letters. No doubt she wanted a more inclusive interest. But Keats felt her beauty so intensely because it was for him a concrete instance of that universal power which so possessed him when he saw it in existence:

> Why may I not speak of your Beauty, since without that I could never have lov'd you – I cannot conceive any beginning of such love as I have for you but Beauty. There may be a sort of love for which, without the least sneer at it, I have the highest respect, and can admire it in others: but it has not the richness, the bloom, the full form, the enchantment of love after my own heart.[7]

But Keats was by no means always in this swooning mood. At this time he was not passing a day, he says, 'without sprawling some blank verse or tagging some rhymes'.[8] His detestation of modish literary chat made him in fact appreciate all the more Fanny's interest in him as a person rather than a poet, 'and here I must confess, that, (since I am on that subject,) I love you the more in that I believe you have liked me for my own sake and for nothing else – I have met with women whom I really think would like to be married to a Poem and to be given away by a Novel.'[9]

Nevertheless, these two impulses, an intrinsic and constant quarrel in Keats's nature, appear again and again. On the one hand love as an unclenching, dismantling force; on the other the impulse to turn a bright eye on the concrete actualities of existence. For example, on 15 July he speaks of 'the languor I have felt after you touched with ardency',[10] 'you and pleasure take possession of me at the same moment';[11] and on 25 July, 'all I can bring you is a swooning admiration of your Beauty . . . I have two luxuries to brood over in my walks, your Loveliness and the hour of my death,'[12] and again, 'I hate the world: it batters too much the wings of my self-will, and would I could take a sweet poison from your lips.'[13] On the other side we have this marvellously creative and often comic observation of the world:

> Tomorrow I shall, if my health continues to improve during the night, take a look fa[r]ther about the country, and spy at the parties about here who come hunting after the picturesque like beagles. It is astonishing how they raven down scenery like children do sweetmeats.[14]

Sometimes the rocking imbalance of these two dispositions of the poet is corrected by a calmer, more central pressure. In the letter written from Winchester, where he went with Brown on 12 August, and which he liked so much both because of its beautiful cathedral and ancient buildings, and also because his little coffin of a room at Shanklin had been changed for a larger one, we see both the positive and the negative in his nature as well as the third, steadying influence. The positive side appears in his quick, crisp account of a near accident witnessed near Southampton:

> There came by a Boat well mann'd; with two naval officers at the stern – Our Bow-lines took the top of their little mast and snapped it off close by the bord – Had the mast been a little stouter they would have been upset – In so trifling an event I could not help admiring our seamen – Neither Officer nor man in the whole Boat moved a Muscle – they scarcely notic'd it even with words.[15]

This sharply noted incident is immediately followed by that other, untethering and indulgent bias, 'it seems to me that a few more moments thought of you would uncrystallize and dissolve me'. But in the body of the letter we see the poet occupied with the substance and significance of his art:

> I would feign, as my sails are set, sail on without an interruption for a Brace of Months longer – I am in complete cue – in the fever: and shall in these four Months do an immense deal – This Page as my eye skims over it I see is excessively unloverlike and ungallant – I cannot help it – I am no officer in yawning quarters: no Parson-romeo – My Mind is heap'd to the full; stuff'd like a cricket ball – if I strive to fill it more It would burst – I know the generallity of women would hate me for this; that I should have so unsoften'd so hard a Mind as to forget them; forget the brightest realities for the dull imaginations of my own Brain – But I conjure you to give it a fair thinking; and ask yourself whether 't is not better to explain my feelings to you, than write artificial Passion – Besides you would see through it – It would be vain to strive to deceive you – 'T is harsh, harsh, I know it – My heart seems now made of iron.[16]

On 5 September he collected some seventy pounds from Hessey and Haslam. He had now completed 'Lamia' and was revising 'St Agnes'. When he hurried into town in the middle of September, summoned by a letter from George whose financial affairs were in a parlous way, he reported that he could not trust himself to visit Hampstead: 'If I were to see you to day it would destroy the half comfortable sullenness I enjoy at present into downright perplexities.'[17] On 15 September he returned to Winchester and composed what is by general agreement his greatest poem, 'To Autumn', on the nineteenth. By 21 September he had finally abandoned *The Fall of Hyperion*. He returned to London on 8 October to lodgings in Westminster, and on 10 October he visited Fanny Brawne.

It is clear from letters written on 11 and 13 October that Fanny's effect on him, when he did see her, was shattering. He is both totally absorbed by her and deeply disturbed:

> The time is passed when I had power to advise and warn you against the unpromising morning of my Life – My love has made me selfish. I cannot exist without you – I am forgetful of every thing but seeing you again – my Life seems to stop there – I see no further. You have absorb'd me. I have a sensation at the present moment as though I was dissolving.[18]

George had now returned to London to investigate the problems of their inheritance. Keats saw his brother off for Liverpool on 3 February, and travelled back by stage coach. This was the night of his first severe haemorrhage and the clear indication of an early death.

The romantic blend of love, pain, religion and death, is present in the hectic quality of his language. Keats's experience with Fanny constantly mixed happiness and misery. Their relationship appears to have had very little peace, nothing of serenity:

> You must believe you shall, you will that I can do nothing say nothing think nothing of you but what has its spring in the Love which has so long been my pleasure and torment. On the night I was taken ill when so violent a rush of blood came to my Lungs that I felt nearly suffocated – I assure you I felt it possible I might not survive and at that moment thought of nothing but you – When I said to Brown 'this is unfortunate'. . . .[19]

In the same month the letters suggest both that he has been willing to free Fanny from her engagement and that he is harassed by jealousy: 'My greatest torment since I have known you has been the fear of you being a little inclined to the Cressid.'[20] Increasingly one is aware of misery turning to despair: 'You know our situation – what hope is there if I should be recovered ever so soon – my very health with [will] not suffer me to make any great exertion. I am recommended not even to read poetry much less write it. I wish I had even a little hope.'[21]

Clearly, friends were advising them, as we see in another February letter, not to expect too much in their situation, but as soon as Keats brings himself to something even approaching resignation, his passion belies his acceptance: 'Whatever violence I may sometimes do myself by hinting at what would appear to any one but ourselves a matter of necessity, I do not think I could bear any approach of a thought of losing you.'[22] In moments of recovery, as we see again in the letters of this month, he shows a tenderness and humorous solicitude for Fanny, advising her about 'open doors and windows and going without your duffle grey'.[23] He sits in the front parlour so that he may see her for a moment in the garden of her house. He assures her that to see her happy and in high spirits is a great consolation to him but it is also an occasion of suspicion and anguish. Even the moments when he reports the slightest improvement in his condition have a touch of desperation in them. He is stronger than he was but God alone knows whether he is destined to taste of happiness with her. His doctor's inward knowledge of his illness constantly qualifies even this moderate optimism: 'Indeed I will not deceive you with respect to my Health,' he reports on 24 February. 'This is the fact as far as I know. I have been confined three weeks and am not yet well – this proves that there is something wrong about me which my constitution will either conquer or give way to.'[24] He makes the point, as he reflects on their correspondence, of how much he distrusts the artificiality of most love letters. He had been reading Rousseau's correspondence and disparages 'the perplexed strain of mingled finesse and sentiment in which the Ladies and gentlemen of those days were so clever, and which is still prevalent among Ladies of this Country who live in a state of resoning romance.'[25] One sees here again, too, that touch of sturdy English patriotism that appears in Keats from time to time when he thinks of 'the continual and eternal fence and attack of Rousseau and these sublime Petticoats'.[26] 'Thank God I am born in England with our own great Men before my eyes – Thank god that you are fair and can love me without being Letter-written and sentimentaliz'd into it.'[27] There are moments of weakness and pathos, cries for sympathy: 'Will you come towards evening instead of before dinner – when you are gone, 't is past – if you do not come till the evening I have something to look forward to all day.'[28] And one must not neglect to note Keats's stubbornness and courage in his appalling situation: 'I will be as obstinate as a Robin, I will not sing in a cage – Health is my expected heaven and you are the Houri – this word I believe is both singular and plural – if only plural, never mind – you are a thousand of them.'[29]

This moral valour still shows itself in a dapple of humour, of that brisk and cheerful kind so common in the bulk of Keats's correspondence. 'There's the Thrush again – I can't afford it – he'll run me up a pretty Bill for Music – besides he ought to know I deal at Clementi's.'[30] Or again in March, as he sits strengthless, feverish and wasting, he says that if he were a little less selfish and more enthusiastic, 'I should run round and surprise you with a knock at the door. I fear I am too prudent for a dying kind of Lover. Yet, there is a great difference between going off in warm blood like Romeo, and making one's exit like a frog in a frost.'[31] And then in April, while still insisting that he improves a little every day, he refers to his regimen of resting and starvation with a certain light-heartedness: 'Feeding upon sham victuals and sitting by the fire will completely annul me. I have no need of an enchanted wax figure to duplicate me for I am melting in my proper person before the fire.'[32]

This is among the last evidence of a happier, more generous Keats. In the remaining half dozen letters, which go from May to August, the voice is shriller, the attitude more pinched and suspicious, the tone more angrily exigent and overbearing, the feelings distracted and even spiteful, his self-regard more and more concentrated, the wretchedness sourer, the misery deepening into despair. He cannot bear to be out of her thoughts, or to think of her enjoying herself among others. 'I am greedy of you,' he says. 'Do not think of any thing but me. . . . Your going to town alone, when I heard of it was a shock to me . . . *promise me you will not for some time, till I get better*. . . . You must be mine to die upon the rack if I want you.'[33] We feel increasingly a sense of uncontrolled and indignant diction, accompanied by a neurotic suspicion and sexual jealousy: 'I suspect a few people to hate me well enough, *for reasons I know of, who have pretended a great friendship for me.*'[34] Even in the letters when his frenzy abates, it is rather from weariness than will, one judges. He lies with her ring on his finger and her flowers at his side, as he tells her in June; and he reports at the beginning of July that he is marking the most beautiful passages in Spenser to give her some small pleasure. As soon as his energy revives at all, as it did on 5 July when he went for a walk – July was a fine, sunny month – he begins to rage at Fanny again for her flirting with Brown, '. . . a good sort of Man – he did not know he was doing me to death by inches.'[35]

> For myself I have been a Martyr the whole time, and for this reason I speak; the confession is forc'd from me by the torture. I appeal to you by the blood of that Christ you believe in: Do not write to me if you have done anything this month which it would have pained me to have seen. You may have altered – if you have not – if you still behave in dancing rooms and other societies as I have seen you – I do not want to live – if you have done so I wish this coming night may be my last. I cannot live without you, and not only you but *chaste you: virtuous you*.[36]

He is lacerated by this anxiety about Fanny's virtue:

> Shakspeare always sums up matters in the most sovereign manner. Hamlet's heart was full of such Misery as mine is when he said to Ophelia 'Go to a Nunnery, go, go!' Indeed I should like to give up the matter at once – I should like to die. I am sickened at the brute world which you are smiling with. I hate men and women more.[37]

The closing words are of waste and despair: '. . . every thing else tastes like chaff in my Mouth.' 'The last two years taste like brass upon my Palate . . . the world is too brutal for me – I am glad there is such a thing as the grave.'[38]

A month before this letter, written at the beginning of July, the third volume of poems, *Lamia, Isabella, The Eve of St Agnes and Other Poems*, had been published 'with low hopes' as far as Keats was concerned but, in the event, it received a distinctly more favourable response than his earlier work. It was warmly reviewed by Charles Lamb in the *New Times* and by Francis Jeffrey in the *Edinburgh Review* in August. This was too late to qualify Keats's despair. It was clear to others as well as to himself that the grave was not far off. Certainly another English winter would kill him. He spent the last month in England at the Brawnes's house, nursed by Fanny's mother and by Fanny herself. Shelley, with characteristic but slightly grand generosity, had invited Keats to stay in Italy with himself and his family near Pisa, but Keats did not take up this well-meant offer. He mentioned once or twice in his letters, with the detached indifference of the invalid, that there was a plan for him to spend the winter in Italy. Taylor was approached and advanced the money. Joseph Severn rather than Brown, who was unavailable, undertook to accompany Keats, and Taylor booked a passage for Keats on the *Maria Crowther*, a small ship destined for Naples. He left the Brawnes to stay at Taylor's for a few days before joining the ship at Gravesend. They were unable to sail because of the weather until Monday 18 September. There was, by a perverse irony, a young woman on board, a Miss Cotterell, also in the final stages of consumption. She acted as a terrifying mirror to Keats's own state. The voyage seems to have been plagued with misfortune. Severn wrote about it to Haslam:

> You will like to know how I have managed in respect to self – I have had a most severe task – full of contrarieties – what I did one way – was undone another – the lady passenger though in the same state as Keats – yet differing in constitution required almost every thing the opposite to him – for instance if the cabin windows were not open she would faint and remain entirely insensible 5 or 6 hours together – if the windows were open poor Keats would be taken with a cough (a violent one – caught from this cause) and sometimes spitting of blood – now I had this to manage continually for our other passenger is a most consummate brute – she would see Miss Cotterell stiffened like a corpse [for] I have sometimes thought her dead – nor ever lend [her] the least aid – full a dozen times I have recovered this Lady and put her to bed – sometimes she would faint 4 times in a day yet at intervals would seem quite well – and was full of spirits – she is both young and lively – and but for her we should have had more heaviness – though much less trouble. – She has benefited by Keats advice – I used to act under him. – and reduced the fainting each time.[39]

But disease could not absolutely suppress the old buoyant, intelligent, and generous Keats. As the ship sailed on from Portsmouth he wrote to Brown:

> Even if my body would recover of itself, this would prevent it – The very thing which I want to live most for will be a great occasion of my death. I cannot help it. Who can help it? Were I in health it would make me ill, and how can I bear it in my state? I dare say you will be able to guess on what subject I am harping – you know what was my greatest pain during the first part of my illness at your house. I wish for death every day and night to

> deliver me from these pains, and then I wish death away, for death would destroy even those pains which are better than nothing. Land and Sea, weakness and decline are great separators, but death is the great divorcer for ever. When the pang of this thought has passed through my mind, I may say the bitterness of death is passed. I often wish for you that you might flatter me with the best. I think without my mentioning it for my sake you would be a friend to Miss Brawne when I am dead. You think she has many faults – but, for my sake, think she has not one – if there is any thing you can do for her by word or deed I know you will do it. I am in a state at present in which woman merely as woman can have not more power over me than stocks and stones, and yet the difference of my sensations with respect to Miss Brawne and my Sister is amazing. The one seems to absorb the other to a degree incredible. I seldom think of my Brother and Sister in america. The thought of leaving Miss Brawne is beyond every thing horrible – the sense of darkness coming over me – I eternally see her figure eternally vanishing. Some of the phrases she was in the habit of using during my last nursing at Wen[t]worth place ring in my ears – Is there another Life? Shall I awake and find all this a dream? There must be we cannot be created for this sort of suffering.[40]

The voyage and the very bad conditions on board contributed, Gittings thinks, to shortening Keats's life.[41] Even when the ship arrived in Naples it was put into quarantine because of a suspected outbreak of typhus in London, and the passengers not allowed ashore until 31 October. They travelled to Rome, Keats steadily growing worse. Taylor had arranged for Dr James Clarke to treat Keats in Rome, where they stayed at 26 Piazza di Spagna in a house much patronized by British visitors. Keats seemed to make a slight but, as it proved, false improvement. He was much worse towards the end of December, his blood spitting became worse, and his fever constant. Keats suffered, raved, wasted, despaired, and was even denied the consolation as a trained physician of not knowing what was happening to him. He looked forward to death. He said to Dr Clarke, 'How long is this posthumous life of mine to last?' He used to hold in his hand an oval cornelian that Fanny Brawne had given him as a parting present. On 23 February, Severn reported to Brown:

> . . . the approaches of death came on. 'Severn – I – lift me up –

> I am dying – I shall die easy – don't be frightened – be firm, and thank God it has come!' I lifted him up in my arms. The phlegm seemed boiling in his throat and increased until 11, when he gradually sunk into death – so quiet – that I still thought he slept.[42]

Notes

1 *Letters*, II, p. 122.
2 ibid., p. 123.
3 ibid., pp. 123–4.
4 ibid., p. 126.
5 ibid.
6 ibid.
7 ibid., p. 127.
8 ibid.
9 ibid.
10 ibid., p. 129.
11 ibid.
12 ibid., p. 133.
13 ibid.
14 ibid., p. 130.
15 ibid., p. 142.
16 ibid., p. 141.
17 ibid., p. 160.
18 ibid., p. 223.
19 ibid., p. 254.
20 ibid., p. 256.
21 ibid., p. 257.
22 ibid., p. 259.
23 ibid., p. 262.
24 ibid., p. 265.
25 ibid., p. 266.
26 ibid.
27 ibid., pp. 266–7.
28 ibid., p. 269.
29 ibid., p. 270.
30 ibid., p. 278. Clementi's was a music publisher.
31 ibid., p. 281.
32 ibid., p. 286.
33 ibid., pp. 290–1.
34 ibid., p. 293.
35 ibid., p. 303.
36 ibid., p. 304.
37 ibid., p. 312.
38 ibid., pp. 312–13.
39 ibid., pp. 354–5.
40 ibid., pp. 345–6.
41 Gittings, *John Keats*, p. 416.
42 Rollins, *The Keats Circle*, vol. II, p. 94.

8
The Odes

The poems with which *Poems*, the volume published in 1820 (and which Keats was almost certainly too ill and depressed to see through the press) begins, 'Lamia', 'Isabella, or the Pot of Basil', 'The Eve of St Agnes', were not written in this order. 'The Eve of St Agnes' was written between 18 January and 2 February in 1819, and revised in September of that year, 'Isabella, or the Pot of Basil' between March and April of 1818 (the unfinished 'Eve of St Mark' was written between 13 and 17 February 1819 but not published till 1848), and Part I of 'Lamia' was written between 28 June and 11 July 1819. It was revised during the second half of August and the beginning of September, and revised again in March of 1820; Part II was written in August and September of that year, after a period spent writing the undramatic drama, *Otho the Great*, in collaboration with Charles Brown. The tradition of poetic drama had been dead too long to allow a revival, even by someone with Keats's gifts, his enthusiasm for the stage, his dramatic imagination, and his profound feeling for Shakespeare. Keats was right to be sure that dramatic poetry was the supreme species of the art; Wordsworth was right to judge that it was no longer possible to write it. 'Isabella, or the Pot of Basil', which was published in 1820, was begun in March 1818 and completed by about 27 April. 'The Pot of Basil', which seems to the modern reader not much more than a feeble nineteenth-century fantasy, was the poetical version of a story told on the fourth day in Boccaccio's *Decameron*. 'Lamia', relying on a myth derived from Burton, with a long history stretching back in English literature to the late fourteenth- or early fifteenth-century *Thomas of Erceldoune*, is certainly meant, unlike 'Isabella', to present a serious idea, the conflict between illusory beauty and the hallucination of pleasure on the one hand, and the clarity of intellect and moral dignity on the other. But there is an excessive disproportion between the serious idea and the academic and literary manner: something one finds again and again in Keats. 'Lamia', says Stillinger, is quite explicit in saying what it is about, namely a 'pessimistic exposition of the dangers of dreaming, of over-investment in illusion, and the impossibility of escape from the realities of the human condition'.[1] I give Stillinger's words in order to stress how significant and cogent the theme of 'Lamia' can be made to seem when one gives an abstract prose paraphrase of it. In fact, in the poem the gap between this attributed importance and the actual existence and movement of the experience is immense. It is a poem, of course, written to the formula of the 'vast idea', plangent and melancholy, presenting not a drama or a reality, but a parable or a tableau. The theme of divine and moral union which Keats is playing with here cannot really be said to command or control the poem, which is no more than an idle anecdote, in the spirit of and no more serious than Burton himself.

What 'Lamia' does show is a pacier gait and a cleaner impact, touches of the drily comic, and a more athletic and vigorous use of the couplet form: effects, surely, of the influence of Dryden whom Keats was now reading. The discrepancy between the vast idea and the richly physical manner and treatment characteristic of Keats is cancelled in 'The Eve of St Agnes', an altogether less pretentious, more unified and more successful poem than 'Lamia'. The demands of the anecdote, slight as it is, drawn from Burton and John Brand's *Popular Antiquities* and infused with the lyrical sensuousness of *Romeo and Juliet*, offered Keats natural opportunities for realizing his extraordinary perception of glow, richness and colour. No doubt we should be right to think also of sources in Keats's personal life, in his sensuous relationship with the sultry Isabella Jones and his youthfully ardent passion for Fanny Brawne. But even if these influences operate in the background, they are wholly absorbed in the actual narrative. When I say 'narrative' I intend to do more than use an elegant variation for 'story'. I have in mind what Wordsworth meant when he claimed in a letter to Coleridge[2] that in the circumstances of the nineteenth century the true voice of the poet was the narrative not the dramatic. First, the reminiscing, self-projecting, ingathering quality of the narrator allows fuller play to the personality of the Romantic poet, that personality which is invariably part of the subject whatever the ostensible theme; secondly, in the narrative form the incapacity of the Romantic and post-Romantic poet to create convincing characters and to embody genuine dramatic action is supplied for by his striking faculty for giving us the immediacy of thought and feeling and the actuality of scene and setting. There is more 'drama', more vivid life and actuality in the lyrical narrative of 'The Eve of St Agnes' than in all the agitation of *Otho the Great* or any other specimen of the closet drama of the nineteenth century. Madeline, delicate and uncharacterized, has neither the depth nor resonance of Juliet, her literary ancestor, but at least she is not simply another example of what Keats called 'the tendency to class women in my books with roses and sweetmeats'. Similarly, Angela, the old nurse beldame, if less racy and more amenable than Juliet's nurse, is just sufficiently outlined to perform a useful function, as indeed is Porphyro, an unspiritual Romeo, and a sensual fantasist. Indeed, it is the setting for these projections of Keats and Keats's reading that has the full glow and bloom of life and actuality. The sexual act, described in an off-putting figure as rose melting into violet, solution sweet, is given nothing like the vigour or the strong physical presence of the window, to take one example.

> A casement high and triple-arched there was,
> All garlanded with carven imag'ries
> Of fruits, and flowers, and bunches of knot-grass,
> And diamonded with panes of quaint device,
> Innumerable of stains and splendid dyes,
> As are the tiger-moth's deep-damasked wings;
> And in the midst, 'mong thousand heraldries,
> And twilight saints, and dim emblazonings,
> A shielded scutcheon blushed with blood of queens and kings.

Here the poet makes us sense with an inner eye the riot of shapes, the thickness of colour and the depth of light, which reflected with its train of religious associations, on to the lovers gives their merely human antics a mythical splendour.

Or another example:

> And still she slept an azure-lidded sleep,
> In blanchèd linen, smooth, and lavendered,
> While he from forth the closet brought a heap
> Of candied apple, quince, and plum, and gourd,
> With jellies soother than the creamy curd,
> And lucent syrups, tinct with cinnamon;
> Manna and dates, in argosy transferred
> From Fez; and spicèd dainties, every one,
> From silken Samarkand to cedared Lebanon.

In these lines we are aware of a certain coolness and crispness as well as a width of reference in the imagery. At the same time there is an observant accuracy in the notation. How exact is azure-lidded, how used and unhectic are blanchèd and lavendered, how solid are the fruits brought from the cupboard, and what strength, both rich and severe, is given to the whole by the oriental and Biblical sonorities of Fez and cedared Lebanon.

Earl Wasserman, who insists on the intellectual, indeed the metaphysical, burden of Keats's Odes, maintains that we have in the modern world lost the understanding of that perspective by which experience in the nineteenth century was ordered into coherence. However dubious we may be about thinking of Keats's Odes as systems of thought, there is no doubt that the modern reader finds a peculiar difficulty in entering into the intellectual and emotional world of the nineteenth-century Romantics. Since the Romantic spirit finally dribbled away in Swinburne, since the total re-ordering of the poetic idiom by Eliot, we now find the poetry of this period, which has a superficial and apparent closeness of relationship to us, more foreign certainly than the eighteenth-century novel or the seventeenth-century poem.

Among the major Odes, 'Ode to a Nightingale', 'Ode on a Grecian Urn', 'Ode on Melancholy' and 'To Autumn', no one has questioned the place and supremacy of 'To Autumn', in which we see wholly realized, powerfully embodied in art, the complete maturity so earnestly laboured at in Keats's life, so persuasively argued about in his letters. In this poem we see firstly the essential nature of the creative poetic activity, and secondly, the justification for seeing the poet, for seeing Keats himself, as the essential literary figure. The poet preserves, while he is acting as a poet, an implacable innocence of the eye: his vision of reality is unclouded by preconception or the cataracts of prejudice. To his uninterrupted sight of the naked object he joins a capacity for expression so densely loaded with the weight of the object that it is much nearer to actual perception than any ordinary description could be. Poetry compares to ordinary thought and speech as the handling of objects compares to algebra. In particular, the poet restores to a perception the emotion which the logical intellect had dropped from it, and in doing so, in re-emphasizing what was ignored, he reinstates the object more completely so that in poetry we get an unusual fullness and volume of experience. To speak of fullness and volume, as we have to in speaking of the ode 'To Autumn', is to imply that while poetry is directly concerned with existences and feelings it is not exclusively concerned with them. If it were, then terms like fullness and volume would be quite improper, and poetry would be an attenuation, not a rendering of experience. Every image, every feeling and every intuition entering a poet's mind is saturated with thought. The combination of pure perception with the thought is what gives poetry its special character, which is to unite concentration and perspective, intensity and scope, and its special effect which is, as Santayana said:

> concentrating and liberating the confused promptings left in us by a long experience . . . we find sweep in the concise and depth in the clear, as we might find all the lights of the sea in the water of a jewel.[3]

The poem has that radical first-hand quality of the best Romantic poets. Nothing, it seems, intervenes between the senses and perception, or between perception and expression, no quirk or bias or myopia or inherited preconception. And of course it has the additional Keatsian virtue of weight, density, volume and massive definition. It is also, as the argument I have just put forward insists, sustained by thought, not thought which is an abstract system or a derivation from prose logic but a concept so deeply identified with the material as to be indistinguishable from it, as a musical idea is from the sound which encloses it. It is a concept of ripeness which is at once a recognition of transience, an acceptance of it and a celebration of its peculiar virtue of fulfilment. Ripeness is now for Keats a varied and balanced concept. The poem offers us the maternal fullness and softness of autumn but also its rougher, acrid side: not only the mellow fruitfulness and the clammy cells, the fume of poppies and the last oozings but also the granary floor, the brook, the cider press, the stubble-plains. Here precisely we find the concentration and liberation Santayana referred to, the sweep, the concision, the depth and the clarity in one of the greatest poems in English.

Earl Wasserman finds a substantial distinction between the 'Ode to a Nightingale' and the 'Ode on a Grecian Urn'. The 'Ode on a Grecian Urn' he considers to be self-contained art, working out its destiny 'in terms of its inherent drama, its own grammar and symbols. Its dynamic force lies within itself and is released and exploited by factors that are the property of poetry alone, and of this poem in particular'.[4] 'Ode to a Nightingale', on the other hand, he considers to be 'synthetically fashioned: instead of operating within its own framework, it functions only because the poet intervenes and cuts across the grain of his materials to make them vibrant. The first is the work of art; the second the workings of art.'[5]

This seems to be an unduly large and over-philosophical way of recording the critic's discovery of a certain poetic impersonality in the 'Ode on a Grecian Urn', which is lacking, or less apparent, in the 'Ode to a Nightingale', where we find the intrusive poet and his private disturbances. But I am sensible of this presence of the poet, as something intrusive and unbalancing, at various places not only in the 'Ode to a Nightingale', but also in the 'Ode on a Grecian Urn' and in the 'Ode on Melancholy'. These poems, with 'To Autumn', represent the crown of Keats's development. They are the poems of a powerful and exquisite sensibility on the point of completing its self-education, on the point of achieving both complexity and coherence, and because of this Keats is liable momentarily to slide into certain deficiencies. But our recognition of these will only make us wonder all the more at the triumph of character which these poems, written at an unpropitious time, represent. It is only natural that there should be slacknesses and patches of unabsorbed personal feeling. The amazing thing is the general quality of control in the Odes, not the occasional relaxation or the very rare collapse. If we look for a moment at the 'Ode on a Grecian Urn', we see there Keats manifesting what Coleridge specified as one symptom of poetic talent, namely the choice of a subject remote from the poet's own private interests. In fact, Keats corrects Coleridge and lights on a subject which is certainly immensely remote from himself, since it is a Greek composite urn with features drawn from several sources, from the Sosibios Vase (now in the Louvre), and from the Townley and the Borghese vases; but also one very close to a purely personal interest, a fascination with classical art. In the same way the metrical technique which combines the formality and elaboration of the grand ode and the uniquely Keatsian management of rhythm joins the order of the impersonal to the rhythms of the poet's individuality. The poem breathes in Keats's way within the space laid down by the regularities of the ode. The statements out of which the poem is made, address, question, generalization, on the other hand, all direct attention towards the object, suppressing in the firmest way the ego-biased first person. The opening stanza establishes – although establishes is too practical and gross a word for the subtlety and imaginative pressure employed – the physical presence of the vase. It brings home to us the paradox of

that existence. It is both a 'still unravish'd bride of quietness' *and* a creature torn with the agitation of men and gods, pursuit and music. The complex embodiment of the urn's being brings together suggestions about the urn's appearance: the carving is so light and delicate that, seeming hardly to touch the vase, it simply haunts about its surface; and suggestions as to its function which is both to express the divine myth and to record and transmit as historian man's engagements with time. The double nature of the urn, blending the serenity of utter peace and the violence of passion – which is the pivot of the first stanza and the source of the rest of the poem – is powerfully confirmed by the deep and varied natural movement of the rhythm: calm, slow and full in the first half, but broken and agitated in the six peremptory and Dionysiac questions with which the stanza concludes. In the same way, the atmosphere so fresh and temperate at the start, becomes hectic and sexually suggestive at the end, developing naturally and without jarring out of the innocence which is called on initially to communicate the sense of the urn's untouched serenity.

Thou still unravish'd bride of quietness,
  Thou foster-child of silence and slow time,
Sylvan historian, who canst thus express
  A flowery tale more sweetly than our rhyme:
What leaf-fring'd legend haunts about thy shape
  Of deities or mortals, or of both,
    In Tempe or the dales of Arcady?
  What men or gods are these? What maidens loth?
What mad pursuit? What struggle to escape?
    What pipes and timbrels? What wild ecstasy?

This poem is packed with examples of that poetic logic which Coleridge said was more fleeting but just as severe as the logic of mathematics. Poetic logic does not argue from a generalization and an application to 'therefore', this, that or the other. It proceeds by a system of inward, sometimes hidden, suggestion, connection and association – which can also include contrast and separation. For example, the first stanza having traced the physical structure of the vase, from its still centre to its turbulent surface, from its existence as a deposit of time to an embodiment of the ideal, makes a shape in the mind, as in the air, moving from peace to violence and from innocence to passion, and by a natural contrasting transposition from an art that is seen to the art that is heard.

In the second stanza the lines:

Heard melodies are sweet, but those unheard
Are sweeter; therefore, ye soft pipes, play on;
Not to the sensual ear, but, more endear'd,
Pipe to the spirit ditties of no tone:

have not only a musical reference but a musical structure, announcing a theme, elaborating it in a middle key, and pointing it in the clear and nimble melodic line of 'Pipe to the spirit ditties of no tone'. Keats uses the word 'therefore' not in an abstract logical way, but with the logic and syntax characteristic of poetry. Indeed, Keats's use of syntax as an instrument of poetic expression is one of his greatest as it is one of the most authentic of the poet's strengths. So that the word 'therefore' in the second line, 'therefore, ye soft pipes, play on', concludes a poetic argument in which silence, having symbolized the timeless and unmoving, is succeeded by music as an expression of activity and passion. Now, the poet reflects, this music is itself never actualized. It is a possibility, a promise implicit in silence. At this point music comes to stand for the perfection of the possible, for all that is superior to the sensual ear. The second half of this stanza and the whole of the third detail this conclusion and connect it with the instances cut in the vase, the fair youth, the trees, the bough, the happy melodist.

Fair youth, beneath the trees, thou canst not leave
Thy song, nor ever can those trees be bare;
Bold Lover, never, never canst thou kiss,
Though winning near the goal – yet, do not grieve;
She cannot fade, though thou hast not thy bliss,
For ever wilt thou love, and she be fair!

Ah, happy, happy boughs! that cannot shed
Your leaves, nor ever bid the Spring adieu:
And, happy melodist, unwearièd,
For ever piping songs for ever new;
More happy love! more happy, happy love!
For ever warm and still to be enjoyed,
For ever panting, and for ever young –
All breathing human passion far above,
That leaves a heart high-sorrowful and cloyed,
A burning forehead, and a parching tongue.

Most readers will have noticed in this third stanza a relaxation of tension, a blurring of the fineness and accuracy of the registration, and a certain hectic and feverish quality. Panting, and cloyed, burning and parching, return too sharply and too immediately to the poet's personal life and indeed, as we must believe, to his bodily symptoms. But Keats, with the resilience of genius, recovers with an extraordinary suppleness and assurance in the next stanza.

> Who are these coming to the sacrifice?
>   To what green altar, O mysterious priest,
> Lead'st thou that heifer lowing at the skies,
>   And all her silken flanks with garlands dressed?
> What little town by river or sea shore,
>   Or mountain-built with peaceful citadel,
>   Is emptied of this folk, this pious morn?
> And, little town, they streets for evermore
>   Will silent be; and not a soul to tell
>   Why thou art desolate, can e'er return.

How marvellously this stanza blends the natural world in 'green altar' with the numinous in 'mysterious priest' and with the traditional piety of ordinary people implicit in the little town and emptied streets. In it, the supernatural and the natural are seen to be stages in an unbroken line. The procession to the shrine, the simple Greek scene leading upward to a more mysterious plane of being, is realized with exquisite lucidity, economy and effect. Similarly, the lowing heifer, the common steaming farm animal, is utterly transformed by her silken garlands into a sacramental victim. And how naturally the emptied town brings up, again with truly poetic logic, the silence investing it, the silence which was a key image in opening and developing the theme. And it is again the image of silence which the poet uses as a means of modulating both the theme and the reader's attention, from the decorated surface of the vase towards its total structure and meaning which hold a permanent significance for mankind. 'Beauty is truth, truth beauty', has been the subject of endless commentary. There is no doubt, as the transcripts of the poem make clear, that the message is meant to be told by the urn to the passer-by, our human representative, us in a projected form. Keats distinguished between fact and truth; it was the business of creative imagination to transfigure the one into the other. And the equivalence of beauty and truth which he asserts here in an elliptical way, is in place at this point in the poem, since this, the transfiguring of brute fact into imaginative or poetic truth, is what the poem has been doing all along. One must quote again the famous remark in his letter to Bailey: 'What the imagination seizes as Beauty must be truth – whether it existed before or not . . . the Imagination may be compared to Adam's dream – he awoke and found it truth.'[6] But the explicitness of the statement in the poem Eliot found to be a blemish and it is difficult to disagree with him. There is something obtrusive and anxious about the last line, even if 'that is all' means this is the most important thing. But Keats's poem is of such stature and reaches such heights that it is perfectly possible for it to sustain and ride imperfections which would have ruined a lesser thing.

The same poetic substance, the same themes in the profoundest sense, which sustain the 'Ode on a Grecian Urn', work through the material of the 'Ode to a Nightingale', which was probably the first of the series of odes written during April and May 1819, the others being the 'Ode to Psyche', and the 'Ode on Melancholy'. Stillinger suggests, appositely but cloudily: 'the structure embraces two dominant tendencies in the literature of his time, the desire to transcend the world of flux and the desire to merge with that world, and it helps explain the way in which both of these contradictory tendencies may exist, as they so often do, in the same work.'[7] Leavis makes the same point but in a characteristically more grappling and tighter way when he speaks of the opposition in the Odes of a heavy drugged movement on the one hand, and a buoyant self-sufficient vitality on the other. He observes in the Odes 'an extremely subtle and varied interplay of motions, directed now positively, now negatively'.[8] John Jones sees the Odes confronting ripeness with what he calls 'withering'. They engage 'the hostility of Keatsian opposites'.[9] Moreover, he says, they turn into poetry the varying forms of space, the intensities of immediate space in the 'Ode to a Nightingale', the calmness of pictured and aesthetic space in 'Ode on a Grecian Urn', and the stretch of real space in 'To Autumn'. For Lionel Trilling the Odes, the supreme achievement of Keats's art, show, like the words he spoke as he lay dying, the tone of the Renaissance, or of Shakespeare himself: '. . . the implicit and explicit commitment to the self even in the moment of its extinction.'[10] These poems, therefore, the conclusion must be, are no more vehicles of ideas as commonly understood than Wordsworth's are carriers of a philosophy. What Keats's Odes show, rather, is, in a phrase of Coleridge, 'the drama of reason . . . the thought growing', where thought means thinking, not the intellectual results but the whole activity, and where, in thought, we include not simply pure intellectual content but all its stubborn wandering roots of feeling, all its flaws of character, all its impurity of motive and all its force of being.

'Ode to a Nightingale', written, according to Brown, one morning after breakfast on scraps of paper under a plum tree in two or three hours – though some have questioned the accuracy of Brown's memory – answers closely to the account just given. We see in it the desire to transcend and to merge with the world of flux and event. We find both buoyancy and a drugged lethargy in the movement. Indulgent relapse towards Lethe is balanced by a clear and open vitality, art as a drug by the breath of life. Ripeness, in fact, in it does confront withering and age. It does explore the feel of space. And it does assert the validity and vitality of self in the face of death. Moreover, the pesonality of Keats is the shaping influence in the poem, so that we find in it both the flaws and the force of that extraordinary being.

The poem begins with the I, or rather the ego, '*my* heart aches . . .', '*my* sense . . .', '*I* had drunk . . .', and progresses by means of a supple system of contrasts to end again with the self – 'my sole self'. When I use the word 'progress' I am thinking of the poem as a journey from one edge of Keats's personality, the mere ego, to the other, the more richly orchestrated self. Both 'progress' and 'journey', however, suggest a process which is serial and successive – and of course the poem and the events in it do occur in time – but the more marked quality of the poem, as indeed of Keats's personality, is not so much change and succession as simultaneity and orchestration. Keats had the gift of maintaining, of preserving within his nature – although these terms may be too passive – of keeping alive what he had outgrown, and of being enriched by what he had discarded. The caressed and indulged child, possessed by the sensuous pleasure of milk, food and warmth, could as he developed make this active sensuality a constituent of adult happiness, and as Lionel Trilling believes, a ground for a more vital and heroic appetite.[11]

In a poetic form analogous to this psychology, then, the dulling opiate and the pull towards Lethe in the first stanza provoke by contrast, but also coexist with, the melodious plot, the shadows numberless and the full-throated ease. The two terms of the contrast, that is, the narcotic and the light-winged Dryad, appear wrestling tensely together. In the second stanza we are given another opiate, wine, but wine which is now cooled, enlivened by the sun, and bringing with it the vitality of dance and song. In the third stanza we have the side of life opposed to dance and sunburnt mirth, fever – a significant term in Keats's personal life – grey hairs, dying youth and leaden-eyed despair. Then in the fourth stanza the nightingale as a separate symbol is abolished and the distance between poet and bird cancelled as Keats identifies himself with the nightingale through the empathic energies of poetry. The paradoxical consequence of this is an even more richly charged response to the immediate setting, and we feel in the soft incense, the embalmed darkness, the packed grass and thickets, a mutual invasion of self and scene. The place itself aspires to the condition of sound; and time is sustained, the past in the fading violet, the future in the coming musk rose, the present in the murmurous haunt of flies on summer eves, and the three coalesce in the instant of identification and ecstasy. In the sixth stanza the theme of disillusion and death is taken up again, not now in its grim or despairing aspects but as something positive to be experienced, something rich, exquisite and intense. But on the very lip of dissolution the poet draws back. 'One thinks ahead', says W. J. Bate with characteristic point and sympathy, 'to Keats's last letter before he left England, when he knew that everything was over. The boat from which he wrote to Charles Brown (30 September, 1820) lay off the Isle of Wight – painfully associated by then with his first ambitious effort, his "test of Invention":

> I wish for death every day and night . . . and then I wish death away, for death would destroy even those pains which are better than nothing. Land and Sea, weakness and decline, are great separators, but death is the great divorcer for ever.'[12]

Death would cancel the efficacy of the symbol for him, and death is transcended in the nightingale's symbolic life. At the end, again with that natural but strangely fleeting logic of poetry, the feel of transcendence brings home to Keats the actuality that must be lived with. But it is an actuality now enlarged and complicated by the significance of the symbol. Actuality + symbol = reality, and the revived and recovered sole-self.

If one turns from considering the poem as a developing organism, and simply looks at it as the reflection of the Keatsian personality, we can see how remarkably inclusive it is in this respect. We have the Romantic fascination with what Coleridge calls the vestibule of consciousness, the drowsy threshold of oblivion. There is the Keatsian capacity to refine from the grossness of taste the subtlety of delight given in the cool and sun-containing wine. Then there is the *memento mori* that Keats's own life constantly flourished in his face, the fever, the palsy, the dying youth. There is poetry thought of as a release from misery, a vehicle to paradise. There is the characteristic lapse that Keats is capable of at any time, even at his most mature, into a slackness of phrasing and discrimination, e.g. 'And haply the Queen-Moon is on her throne, / Cluster'd around by all her starry Fays.' There is also, of course, the characteristic Keatsian strength, the amazingly shaped and filled space which makes up the magnificent fifth stanza. Here sense-experience is a mode of imaginative creation and a most powerful evocation of the fullness of reality. It is immediately followed by that other Romantic fascination, delight in flirting with oblivion, the wooing of death itself. Then there is the use of the nightingale as a symbol, though symbol is too abstract and empty a term for the significance that Keats makes it have as an immortal sign of the consolation of beauty amid the sadness of life. And there is, finally, the Keatsian grasp of a more intricate, worn and experienced reality in the last stanza in which fancy is seen to cheat and deceive and the poet is tolled back – a brilliant reversal from being tolled forward to death – to an ordinary but enriched life, and a common but corrected self.

The 'Ode to a Nightingale', then, is not a philosophical poem, even in a Wordsworthian sense of philosophy, nor does it contain a large discursive or paraphrasable element. Its logical groundwork derives from the richly orchestrated personality of the poet, and its immediate shape is given by the pattern of an event – listening to the nightingale. As the poet listens to the nightingale he is rapt out of his ordinary senses. He has an instant of ecstatic union. He is enriched by the significance of that moment. In blending personality and experience the poem presents an engagement with reality of the kind that we see so often in Keats's own letters. In such experiences an immense range of existence, some elements of which appear positively contradictory to one another, are grappled with, suffused with a strongly original colour, and thrown into a brilliantly new arrangement. The range applies not only to the substance but to the means. Whereas silence and sight are dominant in the 'Ode on a Grecian Urn', here sound and space are the instruments of the poet's sensibility: instruments, one must say, which give an extraordinarily close immediacy to reality. Sight is the sense by which we comprehend the fineness of form whereas the senses of space, hearing and touch give us the immediate texture of experience. It is interesting to note that these are modes of experience which normally succeed one another in the growth of the young child, touch and the sense for textures, which is at the beginning his principal mode of experience, giving way as he grows older to the more distant, more controlled agency of sight. But in Keats the feeling for immediacy and texture was never excluded from his sensibility. It is one of the most glittering examples of his power to keep alive what in others becomes inoperative, and it is a faculty which accounts as much as anything else for the immediacy of impact his poetry makes. It is an immediacy which must account for the capacity of this poem to survive in so fresh and living a way the wearing familiarity to which it is subjected. It has an almost Shakespearean power to survive the damage of quotation.

In speaking of the 'Ode on a Grecian Urn', I noted how in that poem the elaborate stanza form, the variety of modes of statement – address, question, generalization – worked towards achieving distance and control. In that poem the first person was emphatically so much less important than the second and the third. In the 'Ode to a Nightingale', the first person is positively present throughout, and the same means, so overwhelming is this influence, contribute to the intimately personal quality of the poem. They help, as Middleton Murry maintains, 'to elucidate the deep and natural movement of the poet's soul which underlies them':[13] although I would prefer to say the deep, natural and idiosyncratic mood of the poet's soul. The mood, indeed, is that special luxurious indolence which seemed to be a peculiarly productive state of feeling for Keats. In it Keats combines indolence with an extreme vividness of awareness, and a tingling anticipation with a lapsing towards dissolution: alertness with dreaminess, and melting lethargy with electric energy. John Holloway, writing of Keats's Odes, finds the very subject matter to be the turning into poetry of the mood in which Keats writes. The Odes, in this view, are poems about the mood from which Keats's poetry at that time springs, fusing the same 'quiet and wild ecstasy, the same exquisite but precarious balance of grief and happiness, the same eternalization of a passing moment'.[14] He quotes a passage from the letter written on 19 March 1819, which gives Keats's coolest

and most objective, as the most fully rehearsing and enacting, prose account of it:

> This morning I am in a sort of temper indolent and supremely careless: I long after a stanza or two of Thompson's Castle of Indolence – My passions are all asleep from my having slumbered till nearly eleven and weakened the animal fibre all over me to a delightful sensation about three degrees this side of faintness – if I had teeth of pearl and the breath of lillies I should call it languor – but as I am I must call it Laziness – In this state of effeminacy the fibres of the brain are relaxed in common with the rest of the body, and to such a happy degree that pleasure has no show of enticement and pain no unbearable frown. Neither Poetry, nor ambition, nor Love have any alertness of countenance as they pass by me; they seem rather like three figures on a greek vase – A Man and two women – whom no one but myself could distinguish in their disguisement. This is the only happiness; and is a rare instance of advantage in the body overpowering the Mind.[15]

In this passage, turned directly into poetry in the sluggishly unsatisfactory 'Ode on Indolence', we see, on the one side the delicate aesthete – three degrees this side of faintness, with teeth of pearl and breath of 'lillies' – in that exquisite suspension between passivity and activity which concentrates on 'multiplying and saving from the dark gulf, happy moments of consciousness', as Henry James put it in *The Tragic Muse*. On the other side we have a robust Shakespearean energy capable of realizing this attenuated delicacy of feeling with amazing fullness, richness and conviction. One has – as Leavis reminded us – a sense of great power applied to an insufficient subject, a sense of disproportion between the talent and the theme. Goethe, said George Santayana,[16] gives us the immediacy of life treated romantically; Keats gives us the immediacy of personal consciousness treated like an Elizabethan. This condition of consciousness, or rather the over-deliberate and exquisite savouring of it, which was characteristic of Keats and which so much affected later poetry and lesser poets, is a predilection in Keats which the contemporary sensibility unduly encouraged. The power so strongly to embody it, on the other hand, was the more than contemporary and the more than personal gift of a great poet. One of the reasons why 'Ode on Melancholy' seems to me more satisfactory than it does to several other critics, is that the gap between the material and the powers turned upon

it seems much less wide and much less disconcerting. It is a poem which exists at a lower temperature, a lesser intensity of creation. It projects a more contracted universe. When I spoke of Keats giving us the immediacy of consciousness I was thinking not only of his power to render the immediate state of his own consciousness, but of his spontaneous – and if I may put it like this – his unselfconscious way of communicating the whole of his mind, both its strength and weaknesses, its flint and marshmallow: the capacity which delights us in his letters. One of the elements of that consciousness is a decided literary quality or perhaps one should say more largely a decided quality of general cultivation. All these great poems of Keats remind us that although he was not a classical scholar, having little Latin and no Greek, he had a quickness of familiarity with the classical world, at least as it was mediated by Elizabethan translations, as he had with that of the stage and of painting (there are reminiscences of Titian's *Bacchus and Ariadne* and Claude's *Enchanted Castle* in 'Ode to a Nightingale').

This general quality of cultivation is present throughout the poem, whether in the echoes of Burton's *Anatomy of Melancholy* or of Shakespeare's sonnets, even in the rejected first stanza which has a grotesque *grand guignol* air about it.

> Though you should build a bark of dead men's bones,
> And rear a phantom gibbet for a mast,
> Stitch creeds together for a sail, with groans
> To fill it out, blood-stained and aghast;
> Although your rudder be a dragon's tail
> Long sever'd, yet still hard with agony,
> Your cordage large uprootings from the skull
> Of bald Medusa, certes you would fail
> To find the Melancholy – whether she
> Dreameth in any isle of Lethe dull.

Melancholy is seen in the poem as a positive and creative influence, a condition of creation, as it was in the passage quoted just now from the letters. It is not simply to be associated with the narcotic and conventional symbols of negation which fill the first stanza, but rather to be seen as an element both in direct, sensual experience and in the mature and more realistic appreciation of passage and transience. (And, of course, sadness is surely very much in place in one approaching this theme in the psychological and physical condition in which Keats found himself.) The poem traverses a remarkable range of symbol, from the conventional Elizabethan kind in the first stanza to the fresh, natural kind in the second, and to the cloudier but none the less individually characterized personifications in the third. And we see again the peculiarly Keatsian paradox of the powerful physical evocation of thin and wavering states of feeling. In the melancholy fit which drowns the soul, one is to glut one's sorrow, feed upon beauty, while a strenuous tongue must burst joy's grape. Keats's judgement in cancelling the first macabre stanza cannot, I think, be faulted, although some, for example Harold Bloom,[17] think it weakens the poem. As it stands, and without these lines, the poem is surely more coherent and more of a piece within itself.

This poem is like a languorous caress, perfect in its way and place but not to be accounted the sum of human wisdom. Out of it comes much that marked and debilitated the later poetry of the nineteenth century: such tendencies, for example, as taking poetry to be a magic garden or palace of art, or a refuge from the grimmer realities of life; or a tendency to view poetry as a semi-religious, non-rational therapy for the senses, as in Swinburne; or the tendency, more largely, to see not only literature but life itself as an aesthetic object, the habit of thought we observe in Virginia Woolf, the most gifted and poetic of the Bloomsbury Group. The mistress's anger in the 'Ode on Melancholy' is not a real emotion with a warrant in life and a power to evoke a cogent response. It is little more than part of an object, a thread in a composition designed to satisfy an aesthetic observer. Much in the 'Ode to Psyche', perhaps the least regarded of the Odes, although it was explicitly selected for approval by T. S. Eliot, illustrates the account just given. The 'Ode to Psyche' presents us with poetry felt to be a waking dream, with a classical apparatus as mediated by Spenser and Milton and with Keats's favoured evolutionary interpretation of the Pantheon – Psyche is the latest and most highly evolved form of the divine – and with all the associations of poetry as a surrogate religion or ritual:

> So let me be thy choir, and make a moan
>   Upon the midnight hours;
> Thy voice, thy lute, thy pipe, thy incense sweet
>   From swinged censer teeming;
> Thy shrine, thy grove, thy oracle, thy heat
>   Of pale-mouth'd prophet dreaming.

Yes, I will be thy priest, and build a fane
  In some untrodden region of my mind,
Where branched thoughts, new grown with pleasant pain,
  Instead of pines shall murmur in the wind:
Far, far around shall those dark-cluster'd trees
  Fledge the wild-ridged mountains steep by steep;
And there by zephyrs, streams, and birds, and bees,
  The moss-lain Dryads shall be lull'd to sleep;
And in the midst of this wide quietness
A rosy sanctuary will I dress
With the wreath'd trellis of a working brain,
  With buds, and bells, and stars without a name,
With all the gardener Fancy e'er could feign,
  Who breeding flowers, will never breed the same:
And there shall be for thee all soft delight
  That shadowy thought can win,
A bright torch, and a casement ope at night,
  To let the warm Love in!

But, as we see in the last stanza of this poem which Kenneth Allott claimed illustrated 'better than any other Keats's possession of poetic power, in conjunction with what was for him an unusual artistic detachment',[18] there is more in 'Ode to Psyche' than premonitions of Tennyson, Arnold and Swinburne. There is, for instance, that special Keatsian version of the general Romantic power to establish a filled and living landscape and to make that a perfect context and analogue for the movement of his own thought – to place 'in the midst of this wide quietness . . . the wreath'd trellis of a working brain'/If the Ode 'To Autumn' has to do with the fully embodied present, and the 'Ode to a Nightingale' and 'Ode on a Grecian Urn' with recovering moments and instances of perfection and holding them against the attrition of time and the encroachment of age and misery, the 'Ode to Psyche' is directed – but with what tragic irony – to a willed and confident future. In what is simultaneously vision and determination Keats makes imagination, seen as both an activity and the results of that activity, clear a space and be a space in the crowded world for recovery and revival while it also powerfully multiplies and creates possibilities of the ideal. How balanced and inclusive a cast of thought, what maturity of sensibility is conveyed by combining, as Keats does, the withdrawal and passivity of the 'rosy sanctuary' with the robust potency of the gardener: 'Who breeding flowers, will never breed the same.' This is the Keatsian imagination which, like Adam's, awakes and finds the truth, which preserves sensuality while refining it into sensibility, and which, realizing the great theme of Keats's artistic and personal life, schools an intelligence and makes it a soul. The Odes are the body and the expressed life of that complex, troubled and splendidly human creation, the Keatsian soul.

Notes

1 Stillinger, *The Hoodwinking of Madeline*, p. 53.
2 To S. T. Coleridge, 19 April 1808.
3 *Three Philosophical Poets*, pp. 123–4.
4 Earl R. Wasserman, *The Finer Tone* (Baltimore: Johns Hopkins Press, 1953), p. 179.
5 ibid.
6 *Letters*, I, pp. 184–5.
7 Stillinger, *The Hoodwinking of Madeline*, p. 103.
8 F. R. Leavis, *Revaluation*, p. 246.
9 Jones, *John Keats's Dream of Truth*, p. 222.
10 Lionel Trilling, *The Opposing Self* (London: Secker & Warburg, 1955), p. 48.
11 Cf. ibid., p. 33.
12 Bate, *John Keats*, p. 508.
13 Middleton Murry, *Keats and Shakespeare* (London: Oxford University Press, 1925), p. 129.
14 John Holloway, 'The Odes of Keats', in *Critics on Keats*, ed. Judith O'Neill, p. 66.
15 *Letters*, II, pp. 78–9.
16 *Three Philosophical Poets*, p. 181.
17 Harold Bloom, *The Visionary Company* (London: Gollancz, 1961), pp. 403–6.
18 Kenneth Allott, 'Keats's Ode to Psyche', in *Critics on Keats*, p. 89.

Select bibliography

John Keats *Poems*, London: C. & J. Ollier, 1817.
Endymion, London: Taylor & Hessey, 1818.
Lamia, Isabella, The Eve of St. Agnes, and Other Poems, London: Taylor & Hessey, 1820.

Abbott, Claude Colleer (ed.), *The Correspondence of G. M. Hopkins and R. W. Dixon*, London: Oxford University Press, 1935.

____ *The Further Letters of Gerard Manley Hopkins*, London, New York, Toronto: Oxford University Press, 1938.

Allott, Kenneth, 'Keats's Ode to Psyche', in Judith O'Neill (ed.), *Critics on Keats*, London: Allen & Unwin, 1967.

Allott, Miriam, *The Poems of John Keats*, London: Longman, 1970.

Arnold, Matthew, *Essays in Criticism*, London: Macmillan, 1888.

Barnard, John, *John Keats: The Complete Poems*, Harmondsworth: Penguin, 2nd edn, 1976.

Bate, Walter Jackson, *John Keats*, Cambridge, Mass.: Harvard University Press, and London: Oxford University Press, 1964.

Beal, Anthony (ed.), *D. H. Lawrence: Selected Literary Criticism*, London: Heinemann, 1955.

Bloom, Harold, *The Visionary Company*, London: Gollancz, 1961.

Coburn, Kathleen (ed.), *Inquiring Spirit*, London: Routledge & Kegan Paul, 1951.

____ *The Letters of Sara Hutchinson, 1800–1835*, London: Oxford University Press, 1954.

Coleridge, Ernest Hartley (ed.), *The Poems of Samuel Taylor Coleridge*, London: Oxford University Press, 1927.

Coleridge, Samuel Taylor, *The Friend*, London: Bell, 1875.

____ *Table Talk*, London: Walter Scott, 1894.

____ *Biographia Literaria* (ed. J. Shawcross), 2 vols, Oxford: Clarendon

Press, 1907.
Colvin, Sir Sidney, *John Keats: his Life and Poetry, his Friends, Critics, and After-fame*, London: Macmillan, 1917.
Eliot, T. S., *The Use of Poetry and the Use of Criticism*, London: Faber & Faber, 1933.
Finney, C. L., *The Evolution of Keats's Poetry*, 2 vols, Cambridge, Mass.: Harvard University Press, 1936.
Garrod, H. W., *Keats*, Oxford: Clarendon Press, 1926; revised edn, 1939.
____ *The Poetical Works of John Keats*, Oxford Standard Authors series, Oxford: Clarendon Press, 1956.
Gittings, Robert, *John Keats*: The Living Year, London: Heinemann, 1954.
____ *The Mask of Keats*, London: Heinemann, 1956.
____ *John Keats*, London: Heinemann, 1968.
Griggs, E. L. (ed.), *Collected Letters of Samuel Taylor Coleridge 1785–1806*, 4 vols, Oxford: Clarendon Press, 1956–9.
Halévy, Eli, *A History of the English People in the Nineteenth Century*, London, 1926; 2nd, rev. edn, London: Benn, 1949.
Jack, Ian, *Keats and the Mirror of Art*, Oxford: Clarendon Press, 1967.
Jones, John, *John Keats's Dream of Truth*, London: Chatto, 1969.
Knight, G. Wilson, *The Starlit Dome*, London: Oxford University Press, 1941.
Leavis, F. R., *Revaluation*, London: Chatto, 1936.
Leavis, F. R. and Q. D., *Dickens the Novelist*, London: Chatto, 1970.
Mann, Thomas, *Doctor Faustus*, Harmondsworth: Penguin, 1968.
Milnes, R. M. (ed.), *Life, Letters, and Literary Remains, of John Keats*, 2 vols, London: Edward Moxon, 1848.
____ 'Another Version of Keats's Hyperion (i.e. The Fall of Hyperion)', in *Miscellanies of the Philobiblion Society III*, 1856–57.
Murry, Middleton, *Keats and Shakespeare*, London: Oxford University Press, 1925.
O'Neill, Judith (ed.), *Critics on Keats*, London: Allen & Unwin, 1967.
Ricks, Christopher, *Keats and Embarrassment*, Oxford: Clarendon Press, 1974.
Rollins, Hyder Edward, *The Keats Circle*, 2 vols, Cambridge, Mass.: Harvard University Press, 1948.
____ *The Letters of John Keats: 1814–1821*, 2 vols, Cambridge, Mass.: Harvard University Press, 1958.

_____ *The Keats Circle: Letters & Papers 1816–1879*, 2 vols, Cambridge, Mass.: Harvard University Press, 2nd edn, 1965. (Includes the supplementary material published in *More Letters & Poems of the Keats Circle*, 1955.)

Santayana, George, *The Life of Reason*, New York: Charles Scribner's Sons, 1905.

_____ *Three Philosophical Poets*, Cambridge, Mass.: Harvard University Press, 1941.

_____ *Interpretations of Poetry and Religion*, New York: Evanston, and London: Harper & Row, 1957.

Selincourt, E. de, *The Poems of John Keats*, London: Methuen, 1905, 5th, rev. edn, London: Methuen, 1926.

Sharp, William, *Life and Letters of Joseph Severn*, London: Sampson Low & Co., 1892.

Smith, Logan Pearsall, *Little Essays drawn from the Writings of George Santayana*, London: Constable, 1920.

Stillinger, Jack, *The Hoodwinking of Madeline*, Urbana: University of Illinois Press, 1971.

_____ *The Texts of Keats's Poems*, Cambridge, Mass.: Harvard University Press, 1974.

Trilling, Lionel, *The Opposing Self*, London: Secker & Warburg, 1955.

Walsh, William, *The Use of Imagination*, London: Chatto, 1959.

Ward, Aileen, *John Keats: The Making of a Poet*, London: Secker & Warburg, 1963.

Wasserman, Earl R., *The Finer Tone: Keats's Major Poems*, Baltimore: Johns Hopkins Press, 1953.

White, R. J., *Life in Regency England*, London: Batsford, 1963.

Index